MW01252959

The Lost Gospel

The Lost Gospel:
Christianity and Blacks in North America

By

Jerome Teelucksingh

CAMBRIDGE
SCHOLARS

P U B L I S H I N G

The Lost Gospel: Christianity and Blacks in North America,
by Jerome Teelucksingh

This book first published 2010

Cambridge Scholars Publishing

12 Back Chapman Street, Newcastle upon Tyne, NE6 2XX, UK

British Library Cataloguing in Publication Data
A catalogue record for this book is available from the British Library

ISBN (10): 1-4438-1635-3, ISBN (13): 978-1-4438-1635-9

Dedicated to the African Diaspora in the Americas

TABLE OF CONTENTS

LIST OF TABLES

FOREWORD

Jerome Teelucksingh knows how to tell a story with passion and scholarly erudition. In a previous book, *Caribbean-Flavoured Presbyterianism* (2008), he explored the contributions of the Christian educational institutions – of which he is himself a beneficiary – in shaping post-independence Trinidad and Tobago. Now in *The Lost Gospel*, he has focused on the role of the churches in the education of Black Canadians, the development of their leadership and managerial skills, and the origins of Black Theology.

Dr. Teelucksingh does not underestimate or ignore the discrimination blacks experienced in Canada. He notes that prejudice was a determining factor in the decision, after emancipation in the United States, of many to return there, or to Africa. Those remaining in Canada formed numerous self-help organizations including vital Black churches that became the cultural, as well as spiritual focal points of their communities. Dr. Teelucksingh concludes that, by facilitating the assimilation of large numbers of escaped slaves to their new host society, the Christian churches enabled blacks to overcome the trauma and psychological damage of slavery and to adapt to Canadian society.

A young historian in the Department of History at The University of the West Indies, Dr. Teelucksingh captures voices of individuals and groups in a way that communicates a deep respect for the humanitarian efforts of Christians during the struggle against slavery. This study of the interconnection between religion and society recalls words of Joseph as he forgave his brothers, "even though you intended to do harm to me, God intended it for good, in order to preserve a numerous people … so have no fear" (Gen 50:20-21). In ways outlined in this fine study, we see how God provided for a people who, despised and denied fundamental rights, nonetheless overcame and prospered in a new land.

—Paul R. Dekar, Emeritus Professor,
Memphis Theological Seminary of the Cumberland
Presbyterian Church, Memphis, Tennessee.

PREFACE

I'm on my way to Canada,
That cold and dreary land,
The dire effects of Slavery,
I can no longer stand.

Old Master!
Don't come after me-
I'm going up to Canada,
Where colored men are free.

(*Voice of the Fugitive* 15 January 1851)

The history of Blacks departing the United States and settling in Canada is strikingly similar to that of other immigrants in Canada. By the mid-nineteenth century, Canada comprised numerous European immigrants. In the late nineteenth and early twentieth centuries, the Scottish, Hungarians, Italians and Jews initially endured hostile treatment in Canada akin to the Blacks' experiences. These new settlers faced ethnic and religious discrimination and, like the Blacks, were able to overcome these social, religious and cultural obstacles. The European minorities left their homeland to escape poverty, religious or political persecutions; whilst the Blacks wanted to escape the curse of slavery and discrimination.

Despite the study's emphasis on fugitive Blacks and Christianity, it should be acknowledged that not all Blacks in Canada were fugitives. There were some whose guaranteed freedom in Canada did not merit the acceptance of religion or membership in a denomination. However, the work of the Church extended to all Blacks without taking into account their religious conviction. The journey to Canada meant physical freedom but also a liberating experience incorporating the psychological, spiritual and emotional being. The trauma of slavery was still fresh in the minds of many Blacks and many of the answers to their actions and responses can be traced to a violent past and being uprooted from their native Africa. Protestantism provided a much needed support for these refugees seeking spiritual salvation and physical protection.

One of the major objectives of this study is to demonstrate that the relationship between Blacks and religion was essential for their relatively successful assimilation and socialisation in Canada. It also emphasises the work of the Protestant churches in such areas as education, leadership and organisation. A concerted effort was made to capture the voices from the various groups, societies and individuals who were not directly connected to the churches but were influenced by the wave of Protestantism sweeping across Canada in the nineteenth century.

The primary sources for this research included the McCurdy, Strachan and Abbott Papers at the Ontario Archives in Toronto, the Fred Landon Collection and the Canadian Black Studies Project at the University of Western Ontario. These sources provided an invaluable insight into the monumental and diverse contributions of the Protestant churches to the Black community. Useful research centres included the Ontario Black History Society, Shelburne County Genealogical Society, Dalhousie University, Black Cultural Centre for Nova Scotia, Public Archives of Nova Scotia, and the Black Loyalist Heritage Society.

The denominational resources included the United Church Archives at Victoria College and the Presbyterian Church Archives in Toronto. Additionally, the extensive Baptist collection at the Divinity College at McMaster University proved to be a rich reserve of data on the churches belonging to the Amherstburg Association. Such periodicals as the *Amherstburg Courier, Christian Guardian, Voice of the Fugitive, Provincial Freeman* and *Ecclesiastical and Missionary Record* were invaluable storehouses of missionary work in North America.

An explanation of the terminology used in this study will prove useful to the reader. The concept of 'religion' will be defined as the system of beliefs and practices linked to the spiritual nature of worship and having an influence upon the behaviour of individuals. Religion will be seen as a way of examining the relationship between the Black community and the host society. And, the terms 'Protestant' and 'Protestantism' refer to a particular religious orientation inclusive of such Christian denominations as Presbyterian, Methodist, Baptist, Church of England, African Methodist Episcopal (AME), British Methodist Episcopal (BME) and African Methodist Episcopal Zion (AMEZ) who were instrumental in the integration, education or isolation of Blacks. In this work 'Protestant churches' are classified into two groups- Black and White, but this does not necessarily imply two different denominations or practices. Instead the term is used to distinguish the racial composition of congregations and separate institutions.

The term 'enslaved' will refer to 'slaves'. And, 'Blacks' is used in reference to the fugitive and free Blacks from the United States who settled in Canada, and also those free Blacks in the United States. Also, the term 'Black church' will be used to signify congregations/churches comprising Blacks. Similarly, the term 'Whites' will refer to persons of European descent residing in United States and Canada. Until 1841, the province of Ontario in Canada was known as 'Upper Canada' and the province of Quebec was referred to as Lower Canada. During 1841-1867, Upper Canada was known as Canada West and Quebec was identified as Canada East.

At times, this study will incorporate sociological, religious and anthropological concepts in exploring the socio-religious behaviour of Blacks. The use of the term 'acculturation' refers to the exchange of ideas, values, customs, objects and behavior between Blacks and Whites. Likewise, the terms 'integration' and 'assimilation' refer to the processes in which Blacks in Canada or United States acquired unique cultural features and penetrated social institutions of Whites. The concepts of 'adaptation' and 'accommodation' are used to signify changes made by Blacks in adjusting to a new host society. On the contrary, 'segregation' in some Protestant churches, schools and settlements described the separation of Blacks by voluntary or legal means in the nineteenth century.

The main areas of this study dwell on the church's role in education, development of Black leadership, assimilation, theology and independence of Black churches. These themes will be used in reconstructing and investigating the socio-religious encounter between Blacks, from the United States, and Protestants who belonged mainly to the White churches in Canada.

In the Chapter 1 there is mention of early slavery in Canada and the importance of the Underground Railroad in rescuing free Blacks and the enslaved. Chapter 2 emphasised the schisms that emerged among Protestant churches in the United States due to the divisive debate over slavery. There is a concentration in Chapter 3 on the educational nature of the relationship between the Protestant Church and Blacks. This section of the book explored the pre-occupation with education which became the guiding concept in the lives of Blacks. One of the sub-themes is the problems facing Blacks in the public education system and the extent of tolerance at the Sabbath schools. As a result of the provision of educational services, the Protestant Church gained an image as a protector of the Blacks and thereby contributed significantly to their socialisation. In providing education for Blacks, the churches satisfied the educational needs of Blacks and thus provided the basis for a socio-religious relationship with Protestantism.

Chapter 4 focused on the development of Black leadership which involved the transfer of responsibilities and roles from Whites to Blacks.

This theme incorporated the nature and origins of Black leadership and the smooth transition from White to Black leadership. Furthermore, Black leaders extended their work to vigorous evangelistic programs which produced several mission stations that became new bases of religious influence. Chapter 5 explores the extent of the organisational ability of Blacks and the evolution of Black theology. A perusal of church records revealed that comprehensive attempts were made to build a financially and socially stable Black Church in Canada. The experiences of the enslaved and free Blacks in the United States continued to have a strong influence on their activities among the churches in Canada. Additionally, evidence of the association with White churches is seen in the structure and governance of the Black churches.

The final Chapter assesses the church's role in the segregation and assimilation of Blacks. Despite the development of Black leadership, the existence of segregated pews and burial plots indicated the racism in Canada. There is also an analysis of the extent and nature of segregation and assimilation in Canadian society. For instance, the existence of all-Black settlements contributed to the separation of Blacks from the rest of society.

Religion was a key factor facilitating integration, assimilation, adaptation and acculturation among the Blacks. The Wesleyans, Methodists, British Methodists Episcopalians, Baptists and Presbyterians were some of the Protestant denominations instrumental in forging a foundation for the transition to freedom. There will be an attempt to demonstrate the multifaceted role of Protestant churches as Blacks struggled to adapt to their new host society.

In the late twentieth century, the annual celebration of Black History Month coupled with the regular production of films, articles and books on Blacks are an indication of the keen appreciation of their historical presence in North America. An interesting phenomenon that arose in this research is the similarities amongst Black churches in the United States. There was considerable communication between Blacks and Whites which overshadowed the racial problems in society. Those persons interested in Canadian and United States History or sub-fields such as Africana Studies and Black Studies will particularly benefit from this attempt to highlight the religious aspect of the life of Blacks in Canada.

ACKNOWLEDGMENTS

Firstly, I must express gratitude to God for allowing me the strength and wisdom to produce this scholarly work. Also I would like to thank the many librarians, archivists and researchers in Canada and the United States who assisted in locating microfilm, dissertations, articles and obscure books. During my stay in Ontario, the universities, Black societies and historical organisations have been very helpful in providing a suitable environment for research. These include the personnel at the University of Western Ontario Archives, Black History Society and the Metropolitan Library in Toronto.

A special word of thanks to my friends in Canada- the Ashbys and Mohans. They supported and believed in my dream of recording the history of Blacks and religion in Canada. I am grateful to Mrs. Maria Peter-Joseph, History Secretary at UWI and Albert Joseph for assisting with the formatting of the manuscript. Also, the advice of Professor Brinsley Samaroo must be acknowledged. Finally, and most importantly, I owe a debt to my family who provided me with emotional support throughout this research. They provided reassurance during a period of personal struggle as a young historian.

LIST OF ABBREVIATIONS

AMEZ	African Methodist Episcopal Zion
AMA	American Missionary Association
AME	African Methodist Episcopal
AO	Archives of Ontario
AUBA	African United Baptist Association
BME	British Methodist Episcopal
CBA	Canadian Baptist Archives
PCA	Presbyterian Church Archives
SPG	Society for the Propagation of the Gospel
UCA	United Church Archives
US	United States

CHAPTER ONE

FLEEING CRUCIFIXION:
MIGRATION TO CANADA

All who are under the yoke of slavery should consider their masters worthy
of full respect, so that God's name and our teaching may not be slandered
(Timothy 6: 1).

The early enslaved persons were First Nations or indigenous peoples
known as panis. In 1501, Gaspar Corte-Real, a Portuguese explorer,
landed in Newfoundland. He subsequently captured and enslaved 50
native persons. Almost three decades later, in 1535, Jacques Cartier, a
French explorer, captured 10 members of the Iroquois and carried them to
be displayed in France.

One of the earliest known enslaved Blacks in Canada was Olivier Le
Jeune in 1632. He was born in Madagascar, Africa and as a child was
captured by the traders of the enslaved. Subsequently, Le Jeune was given
to the Kirke brothers in Québec. In 1632 the Kirkes decided to sell him
and depart for Britain. This action was prompted by the Treaty of St.
Germain-en-Laye in which Québec was returned to France. The young
slave was educated by Father Paul le Jeune of the Society of Jesus, who
recounted, "...the other day I had a little Savage on one side of me, and a
little Negro or Moor on the other, to whom I taught their letters."[1]

The Dominicans, Franciscans and Jesuits possessed enslaved persons
and ensured they were well-treated. These religious orders neither
condemned nor promoted slavery. By 1720, the clergy in New France
owned 43 enslaved persons and this arose from the fact that, "Slavery was
a social reality, and as such the church accepted it."[2] Even though the
Roman Catholics condemned slavery they felt that persons who were
slaves had experienced bad-luck.[3] Enslaved Canadians were fortunate that
they were not harshly treated as their counterparts in the Caribbean and the
United States. The Canadian economy did not depend on enslaved labour
and thus their population remained relatively small.

There was an early Black presence in Nova Scotia. In a census of
1686 when the French possessed Acadia, a free Black resided at Cape

Sable near Yarmouth. He was identified as "la Liberté, le neigre" (Liberty the Black).[4] In the *Halifax Gazette* of 1752, there was an advertisement for Blacks to be sold to the public.[5] Likewise, in 1775, the *Nova Scotia Gazette and Weekly Chronicle* advertised "A lively, well-made, negro boy, about 16 years old."[6]

In Canada a few of the enslaved persons assisted in the fields but most served as household servants and resided with their masters. Some of the enslaved from Bermuda worked on fishing ships in Newfoundland in the late eighteenth century.[7] In Upper Canada during the 16th and 17th centuries, slavery was common. The enslaved were owned by many of the important British families. This occurred even after 1797, when Lieutenant-Governor John Graves Simcoe of Upper Canada outlawed importation of the enslaved into Upper Canada.[8] Even though slavery was not completely abolished, Canada was the first British colony to pass such a law against slavery.

The enslaved population in Canada gradually increased by the late seventeenth century. On 1 May 1689, Louis XIV allowed the enslaved from the Caribbean to be imported into New France, and in 1709 slavery in the colony became legal. The French needed enslaved persons due to the frequent shortage of labour.[9] The treatment of the enslaved was determined by the Code Noir even though it was never officially proclaimed in New France.[10] Robin Winks believed the enslaved of New France, especially the Blacks, were not severely treated, "They were, after all, expensive and intimately connected to the household as domestics."[11] Some of the enslaved were utilised in agriculture.

Some of the enslaved were even allowed, by the Church, a certain degree of equality as they could be baptized, married, participated in communion and buried under Christian rites. The scarcity of enslaved persons made them expensive commodities. Many attempted to escape to nearby forests or southwards into the Northwest Territory. There were also unpleasant instances as in Montreal in 1734, an enslaved girl, Marie-Joseph Angelique, burned the home of her mistress while attempting to escape. The fire spread and damaged almost half of Montreal. She was found guilty, tortured and hanged in downtown Montreal.[12]

Due to intermittent naval warfare, the risky routes were not used for shipping the enslaved to New France. Marcel Trudel estimated that by 1759 there were 3,604 enslaved persons in New France (1,132 were Blacks) whilst Robin Winks believed the colony had an enslaved population of 4,000.[13] In 1763, the Treaty of Paris resulted in France ceding her lands east of the Mississippi to Britain. The result of this land transfer meant English civil and criminal laws were adopted in Québec and the enslaved were no longer protected under provisions of the Code Noir.

In the aftermath of the American Revolution of 1776, some American settlers opted to migrate with the enslaved, which they owned, to Canada.[14] These settlers eventually resided in areas in Nova Scotia such as Amherst, Liverpool and New Glasgow. The enslaved, belonging to the settlers, had a work regimen which included building ships, cutting wood and clearing fields. Often the enslaved in Canada were those who arrived with their masters. Rev. James Scovil and his family arrived in New Brunswick in 1788. His enslaved persons accompanied him to the province and he ensured they were well-treated after he died. Two of Scovil's servant boys (10 and 12 years old) were bequeathed to his wife, in a will which stated: "that at the age of 26 years they shall be set at liberty provided they do faithfully discharge the duties of servants until that period, and do appoint my son Elias Scovil, and my said wife, their overseers to see that they are reasonably treated."[15]

In Jamaica, in the British West Indies, the Maroons or runaway Blacks proved to be troublesome and a burden for the colonial authorities.[16] As a result, the Jamaican Legislative Council voted that the maroons be sent to exile. The Jamaican government obtained 5,000 acres of land and spent £3000 for buildings in Nova Scotia. Also, the Governor of Nova Scotia applied to the British government for assistance. In July 1796, in a historic trip, 550 Trelawny Maroons were deported to Nova Scotia. Britain agreed to provide an annual sum of £240 "to support a school, and to provide instruction for them in the principles of religion."[17] The moral and religious nature of the maroons proved to be a contentious issue, "They were not christians (sic), they had little idea of any kind of religion. They believed in Acompang, whom they called the God of Heaven. They had no marriage ceremony. A man had as many wives as he chose to support...."[18] Whilst in Nova Scotia, the maroons were exposed to education and religion. James Lockett in "The Deportation of the Maroons of Trelawney Town to Nova Scotia, Then Back to Africa," argued that the inability of the British to defeat the Maroons was one of the reasons why Britain decided to end slavery in 1833.[19]

Migration and Black Presence

Canada received an influx of Blacks as a result of earlier migrations following the American Revolution in 1776, War of 1812 and deportation from Jamaica.[20] On 19 October 1781 the defeat of Lord Charles Cornwallis at Yorktown created a dilemma for thousands of supporters of

Britain. Among those persons departing New York were a few thousand formerly enslaved Blacks who had been encouraged to leave their masters and pledge allegiance to Britain in the hope of attaining protection and freedom.[21]

Among the United Empire Loyalists of 1783, almost 10% were Blacks.[22] From 1782-1784, Nova Scotia welcomed the arrival of 3,548 free Blacks and from this total 1,521 were assembled together in Shelburne.[23] Most of the Black Loyalists were not church-going Christians and whilst enslaved in the United States they were deliberately denied religious teaching.[24] During this time 1,232 enslaved Blacks were sent to Nova Scotia, with 441 being shipped to New Brunswick and 26 for Prince Edward Island.[25] There was a considerable Black presence in Nova Scotian towns as Birchtown, Digby, Granville and Annapolis (see Appendices A and B). During the late 18th century, most of the Blacks had joined churches such as Christ Church in Nova Scotia. By 1798, Upper Canada had 40 Black settlements.[26]

Most of the historiography on Blacks in Nova Scotia mentioned Colonel Bluck as being in command of the "Black Pioneers."[27] Barry Cahill offered a revisionist viewpoint in "Stephen Blucke: The Perils of Being a "White Negro" in Loyalist Nova Scotia" and sought to clarify the misconceptions surrounding one of the province's prominent Blacks. Firstly, Captain Blucke was neither attached nor served as an officer in the "Black Pioneers" which was the only Black Loyalist provincial corps that provided regular military service. Blucke was secretary to the last British commandant of New York City- Brigadier-General Thomas Mulgrave, who had recently served in the West Indies. Cahill contended that Blucke was not a mulatto but "a full-blooded West Indian of African descent."[28] Additionally, Blucke was the only Black Loyalist who received a 200 acre grant of land.

The War of 1812 was the result of the British Navy capturing men and banned goods from United States ships. This coupled with the demands of "War Hawks" in the United States Congress, to conquer Canada, contributed to the United States Congress declaring war against Britain on 19 June 1812. By May 1814 a noteworthy number of Blacks in the North American colonies had voluntarily enlisted in the British forces. Correspondence from the British officers proved the previously enslaved persons had the ability to engage in warfare, "The new raised Black Corps the Colonial Marines gave a most excellent specimen of what they are likely to be. Their conduct was marked by great spirit and vivacity and perfect obedience."[29]

In the Rebellion of 1837, many Black Canadians who were free or refugees courageously defended the province.[30] They served as gunners, soldiers, informants and officers in independent units referred to as "Coloured Volunteers." The name was changed to "Coloured Corps" and they were attached to the Upper Canada militia until it was eventually disbanded in 1850. This division was one of the early instances of racial segregation in a public institution.

Among the early Black population in Upper Canada were men such as Richard Pierpoint (1774-1838) who was born in Senegal, Africa. At the age of sixteen he was captured, enslaved and shipped to New York in 1760 where he was sold to a British officer. Pierpoint (also known as Captain Dick) fought in the American Revolutionary War in a special corps known as the "Butler's Rangers." He also bravely fought in the War of 1812 as "the first colored man who proposed to raise a Corps of Men of Color on the Niagara Frontier...." And, almost a decade later in 1821 was described by N. Coffin, a high-ranking White militia officer, as "a faithful and deserving old Negro."[31]

On 21 July 1821, Pierpoint submitted a petition to Lieutenant Governor John Simcoe requesting a return to his native land of Africa. This was a request similar to one which resulted in the emigration of Blacks from Nova Scotia to Sierra Leone. The cost of such a venture would have certainly not appealed to colonial authorities and Pierpoint's request was rejected. Instead, Pierpoint and ten Black families were given land grants in Garafraxa (located on the outskirts of present-day Fergus). Pierpoint's leadership provided stability to the small community. Soon after his death in 1838, Scottish planters purchased the land and the Black families in Garafraxa gradually dispersed.

Free Blacks in Upper Canada included William Groat, born at Stoney Creek in 1820 and the Hisson family who settled in the Newmarket area during the early 1800s.[32] Wellington County had a rich history of Black settlements during the Loyalist era. Blacks, who mostly settled in the lower part of Peel Township in Wellington County, represented 10% of the total Loyalist emigration from the United States.

In 1833, one of the colonisation schemes propounded by Dr. Thomas Rolph, involved transplanting Blacks from Canada to the island of Trinidad, in the West Indies. But, after eight years of dilly-dallying the plan never bore fruit, mainly due to strong opposition from the Colonial Secretary. In 1844, an advertisement in the *Chatham Gleaner* encouraged Blacks from Upper Canada and Quebec to emigrate to another British West Indian island- Jamaica. By 1861 another proposal surfaced, encouraging the emigration of Blacks in Chatham to Africa and like

Rolph's plan, it never materialised. Such ideas stemmed from the belief that Canada was an inhospitable place for Blacks due to the cold weather and discrimination. The masterminds behind these grandiose schemes were neither segregationists nor biased against the Blacks but some were genuinely sympathetic to the misfortunes and treatment of the fugitives. These aborted ventures reflected the church's shortcomings in addressing the injustices faced by Blacks.

Other Blacks who adopted Canada as their home included Joseph Armstrong, an enslaved who was born in Maryland. In 1837, Armstrong escaped to Upper Canada, settled in Brantford and eventually moved to Peel Township where he began a life in agriculture. Also, there was Henry Lawson, originally from Ghana, West Africa, who was enslaved and made the trip across the Middle Passage. Lawson later toiled on a plantation in Virginia in the United States. He later escaped to Canada.[33] Likewise, John Jenkins, a 24 year old enslaved from Virginia, was a fugitive in Canada and later settled on Brock Road in West Flamboro.[34] Whilst in Canada he purchased, for $850 and $400, the freedom of his daughters who were enslaved in the United States. In 1844, Thomas E. Knox, a free Black from Pennsylvania, emigrated to Canada and established a farm at Queen's Bush settlement. Similarly, Joseph Mallott, an ex-enslaved person from Alabama, became a cook on a Mississippi riverboat which enabled him to purchase freedom. Mallott's migration to Bloomingdale in Woolwich Township was temporary because in 1835, following the birth of his son, his family relocated to Peel Township.[35] During the 1840s, Blacks in Garafraxa sold their land to incoming Scots and eventually dispersed.

Among the early Black families there was a considerable amount of internal migration in Upper Canada. In one instance, Blacks moved from Niagara to Grey County and Fergus but problems arose because they lacked registration papers. This forced some Blacks to become squatters whilst others moved to nearby locations. Evidence of the Black community that once existed in Grey County included the names "Negro Creek" and the small "negro lakes." Similar evidence of migratory patterns is evident in the history of the Durham Road community which survived until many Blacks moved to Collingwood to work in the shipyards during the 1890s.

There were isolated pockets of Blacks in the Artemesia Township in Priceville and there is also evidence that Blacks once existed in the small villages of Pamona, Latona and Yeoville.[36] Fugitive slaves in the Peel and Wellesley Townships comprised some of the first farmers in these districts and it was estimated that between 500 to 900 Blacks once inhabited this region.[37] During 1860-1875, there were Blacks in Wallenstein, Yatton and Glenallan (in the lower part of Peel Township in Wellington County).[38]

In other areas of Canada there was a Black presence. For instance, during 1858-1859 some free Black businessmen from San Francisco migrated to Vancouver Island.[39] An estimated 5,000 Blacks settled in Québec during the nineteenth century with most arriving as freed Blacks after slavery ended in the United States.[40] It is difficult to trace the ancestry of these early Blacks. This is due to the fact that there was inadequate record-keeping and also some Blacks intermarried with the English, Americans, French, Irish and other Europeans who were among the pioneers of an emerging community.

Underground Railroad

During the eighteenth and nineteenth centuries, thousands of freedom-seeking enslaved persons and free Blacks from the neighbouring United States escaped via the loose, secret network known as the "Underground Railroad." James Holly, a Black abolitionist, perceived Canada as "a beacon of hope to the slave, and a rock of terror to the oppressor."[41] Those involved in the Underground Railroad were united by their hatred of slavery and courage to hide and assist fugitive Blacks. Railroad terms were successfully used to deceive and confuse the slave-masters and the public. The 'conductors' of the Railroad would have false compartments in carriages and wagons for escaping Blacks.[42] Cellars, farmhouses, secret passages, attics and churches were the 'stations' where abolitionists temporarily hid their 'passengers.' The 'passengers' travelled from such states as Kentucky, Indiana, Ohio, New York, Virginia, Maryland and Michigan. Those involved in the Railroad sang coded spirituals such as "Steal Away to Jesus" and "Wade in the Water, Children." Also, the song "Follow the Drinking Gourd" referred to the North Star and Big Dipper.[43] Among fugitive Blacks who faithfully served on this route were William and Ellen Craft, Lewis Hayden, William Wells Brown and Sojourner Truth.

Terminals for the fugitives included Niagara, Owen Sound, Collingwood, Oro, Sandwich, New Canaan, St. Catharines, Colchester, Buxton, Chatham, Dresden, Dawn, London, Brantford, Wilberforce, Amherstburg, Sarnia and Windsor.[44] Adrian in Michigan was one of the stops in the Underground Railroad from Ohio via Detroit to Windsor in Upper Canada. The newcomers were welcomed by 'freight agents' in Canada.[45] The extent of the religious faith of the enslaved is evident in their biblical associations which reflected the deeply religious nature of the immigrant experience and the extent of suffering under slavery in the United States. They sought refuge in Upper Canada or "The Promised Land." Harriet Tubman, one of the charismatic conductors of the Underground Railroad was affectionately known as "Moses" to her people. Tubman rescued an estimated 300 enslaved persons during her 19 trips on the Railroad. Her threat to slavery was obvious as there was a hefty reward of $12,000 for her capture. Whilst in Canada, Tubman used the BME Church in St. Catharines as a place of worship and this venue was eventually adopted as the Canadian headquarters of the Underground Railroad.[46]

Supporters of this freedom route included the Baptists, Presbyterians, Quakers and Methodists. One of the conductors was "Aunt Laura" Haviland a Quaker missionary who also served as a teacher in the Windsor-based Refugee Home Society. Other Quakers who assisted were Thomas Garrett, Isaac T. Hopper and Lucretia Coffin Mott. The home of Abraham Shadd, in Philadelphia, served as a station on the Railroad. He also sold subscriptions of the abolitionist newspaper- the *Liberator*.[47] In Ohio, the home of Rev. John Rankin sheltered hundreds of fugitive Blacks. Furthermore, a Black, Rev. Henry H. Garnet, hid fugitive slaves in his church and home based in Troy, New York. Likewise, Rev. John T. Moore of the Wesley AME Church utilised his church as a temporary shelter for fugitives. Additionally, proactive individuals as Revs. Stephen H. Gloucester of the Central Presbyterian Church of Color, Daniel Scott of the Union Baptist Church and Walter Proctor of the Mother Bethel Church (AME Church) were linked to the Underground Railroad.[48]

By mid-nineteenth century the Detroit River which was used as a crossing by many Blacks, became increasingly associated with the biblical River Jordan. Under the protective umbrella of religion, the years in the wilderness of slavery would serve as a central force, a potent reminder to give thanks to God for deliverance unto the land of freedom.[49] The fugitives were able to appreciate Canada as a haven.

Josiah Henson, a slave, was born on 15 June 1789 on a farm in Charles County, Maryland, in the United States. He initially had a kind master, Dr. Josiah McPherson, who died and unfortunately Henson's new owner- Isaac Riley, was cruel. Henson became a Christian at eighteen years of age and in the mid-1820s was loaned to Riley's brother, Amos, in Kentucky. For three years, Henson worked in this state and eventually became a licensed preacher of the Methodist Episcopal Church. In 1829, he purchased his freedom but Riley intended to have him sold in New Orleans. In defiance of his master's plan, in October 1830, Henson, his wife and children escaped to Waterloo, Canada.[50]

Henson, as an agent of the Underground Railroad, assisted more than a hundred slaves from the United States to attain freedom in Canada. He was portrayed as the fictional character 'Uncle Tom' in Harriet Beecher Stowe's classic 1852 anti-slavery novel *Uncle Tom's Cabin*.[51] Interestingly, throughout this life, Henson denied he was 'Uncle Tom' but finally admitted this association, at ninety-three years of age, at a lecture at the Park Street Baptist Church in Hamilton. Henson, one of the best known enslaved fugitives had twelve children, and after his death in 1883, his home at Buxton, Ontario was transformed into a museum.

From 1815 to 1860 an estimated 80,000 enslaved persons escaped using the Underground Railroad with more than half fleeing to Canada.[52] The usefulness of the Underground Railroad may have been exaggerated. Most of the slaves escaped through paths along the East Coast or on boats rather than the Railroad routes. Secondly, the slaves who escaped, enjoyed a relatively privileged status and originated mostly from border states where slavery was less common.[53] In retrospect, the Underground Railroad could be deemed "an epic of American heroism."[54]

Apart from the horrors of the slavery system, there were certain political developments in the United States during 1850-1860 which served as an impetus for the migration of Blacks particularly through the Underground Railroad.[55] This meant that citizens were now forced to assist in the capturing of escaped Blacks or be liable to fines or imprisonment.[56] This 1850 Act amended the Fugitive Slave Act of 1793. The new act provided for the appointment of military commissioners to issue warrants for the assistance of citizens in the capturing of fugitive slaves. This endangered the freedom of the runaway Blacks in the free states and made Canada a possible haven.[57] Despite restrictions, almost a year after passage of the Act, the Detroit Vigilance Committee and the Cleveland Vigilance Committee assisted 2,500 Blacks to Canada.

A decline in membership was experienced among churches in the United States after the passage of the Act in 1850. Both Methodists and Baptist churches suffered from diminishing Black congregations as a result of mass departures.[58] Upon passage of the Act, the Colored Baptist Church at Buffalo recorded a loss of 130 members to Canada. Similarly, the Colored Baptist Church at Detroit suffered a loss of 84 members who fled northwards to Canada.[59] Many urban areas in the United States suffered and there was a considerably slow growth in the Black population.[60] By 1860 there was a considerable Black presence in communities in Canada West (see Appendix C).

During 1851-1853, Illinois, Indiana and Iowa passed legislation which persecuted Blacks for settling in these states. Other states as Michigan and

Wisconsin refused to grant voting rights to Blacks.[61] The Kansas-Nebraska Act in 1854 also jeopardised the status of Blacks and contributed to the prevailing pro-slavery sentiment.[62] Three years later, the Dred Scott decision sealed the fate of Blacks desiring freedom and social improvement. In the 1830s, Dred Scott, enslaved person, was the personal property of Dr. John Emerson of St. Louis (who later resided in Wisconsin). In 1846 upon his master's demise, Scott applied for freedom on the basis that his earlier residence in Wisconsin (which through the Missouri Compromise of 1820 had banned slavery from that area) and later in Illinois (slavery was barred from that territory under the Northwest Ordinance of 1787) guaranteed his status as a free person. The ensuing Supreme Court decision on 6 March 1857 declared the Missouri Compromise as unconstitutional and that the enslaved were "beings of an inferior order (with) no rights which white men were bound to respect."

The ruling of the Dred Scott case meant that Blacks were not recognised as citizens of the United States. Also, Blacks were not protected under the Fifth Amendment (Bill of Rights) which stated no person "...shall be deprived of life, liberty, or property without due process of law." Thus, by the late 1850s the migration to Canada became increasingly appealing to Blacks desiring freedom and protection from the clutches of slave catchers. Being a resident in Canada was no guarantee of safety. In 1853, in Elora there was a failed attempt by a man to capture two coloured boys to serve as enslaved persons in the United States.[63]

It is estimated that there were 5,489 fugitives in Canada West by 1848 and by 1852 there was a sizeable coloured population of 30,000 which included fugitives who came prior to 1830.[64] Some researchers have claimed that during 1800 and 1869, almost 30,000 fugitives arrived in Canada.[65] If they entered at a rate of 3,000 annually, then Upper Canada would have 18,000 fugitives –which was more than half of the 1852 census figure of Blacks in Canada.[66] One of the local newspapers reported that "hundreds of them have lately crossed over from Detroit to Windsor."[67] It is estimated that during the ten year period 1850 to 1860, approximately 15,000-20,000 fugitives entered Canada.[68]

Daniel Hill, using censuses and reports of the Anti-Slavery Society, contended that the population of Blacks in Upper Canada increased by 11,000 in a twenty-year period.[69] Despite discrepancies, there is a consensus that after the passage of the Fugitive Slave Law in 1850 the fugitive population in Canada underwent a dramatic increase. In 1850, the Black population in Upper Canada was estimated to be 25,000-30,000.[70] A newspaper suggested that after a decade the coloured population doubled to 60,000 in 1861 and comprised mostly fugitives.[71] This population spurt after 1850 coincided with the rapid spread of Black churches and renewed vigour of the Protestant mission. The plight of the enslaved was indeed most unfortunate as the journey to Canada was accomplished with few personal belongings and meagre financial resources.

New Brunswick in Canada possessed a noteworthy Black population during the nineteenth century. Most of the early Blacks were domestics and some owned barbershops, second-hand stores and restaurants. Cornelius Sparrow, a Black who arrived in New Brunswick via the Underground Railroad, operated a store known as Royal Saloon. It was located on Charlotte Street and he sold oysters, vegetables and fruits.[72]

Many are not aware that Blacks arrived in Canada at periodic intervals in small isolated groups, without family or friends, and not as a homogeneous entity. The incoming Blacks discovered that there was an absence of any kin relationships with the existing scattered Black population in Canada. In Nova Scotia, Blacks were divided into small subcultures and lacked a collective identity.[73] This was not limited to Nova Scotia and Winks accurately noted that there was "no monolithic Negro identity in Canada."[74]

Undoubtedly, religion had an impact upon the Blacks' mores, social behavior, culture, secular groups, institutions and settlements. They arrived in Canada and some openly accepted Christianity as it offered social benefits. It was central in the process of their adjustment to a new society. The bond with Christianity contributed to Blacks being confident, morally sound, spiritually endowed and intellectually advanced. Probably, without the existence of this link with religion, the Black experience in Canada might have been hostile, lonesome and unfavourable. American anti-slavery workers from Elgin and Kent counties dispatched missionaries to assist with the spiritual welfare of recent American emigrants who settled in the Black community of Yatton, four miles north of Elmira.

Among Blacks, the independence of their church, the involvement in education, development of Black leadership and assimilation were inextricably linked. These factors were instrumental in the socialisation of the Blacks during the nineteenth century. Indeed, without the element of assimilation there probably would have been stunted Black leadership, misinterpretations of Scripture, and education being tailored only for Blacks. The integrating efforts of the various Protestant denominations ensured that Blacks would interact with Whites, become effective leaders and be exposed to a sound and basic education.

Considerable organisation and planning was involved in the settlement of Blacks in Upper Canada. In addition to the comprehensive and secretive operations of the Underground Railroad; in Canada, the

White missionaries (assisted by some Blacks) ensured that schools, settlements and churches were organised and functioning for the incoming fugitives and free Blacks.

Notes

[1] Robin Winks, "Negro School Segregation in Ontario and Nova Scotia," *Canadian Historical Review* 50 (1969): 167.

[2] Robin Winks, *Blacks in Canada* (New Haven: Yale University Press, 1971), 13.

[3] Headley Tulloch, *Black Canadians: A Long Line of Fighters* (Toronto: NC Press, 1975), 72. Winks, *Blacks in Canada*, 12.

[4] John N. Grant, *Black Nova Scotians* (Halifax: Nova Scotia Museum, 1980), 6. See Adam Green, "The Future of the Canadian Negro" unpublished paper presented at the African Baptist Association, Halifax, Nova Scotia. September 1904, 6. Green was the pastor of the Zion Baptist Church in Truro, Nova Scotia.

[5] Grant, *Nova Scotians* 6.

[6] Nancy Lubka, "Ferment in Nova Scotia," *Queen's Quarterly* 2 (1969): 214.

[7] Tulloch 77.

[8] Dalton Higgins, "Slaves in Canada," http://www.nowtoronto.com/issues/2001-07-12/news_spread.html (accessed on September 2, 2006).

[9] Fred Landon, "Canada's Part in Freeing the Slave," *Ontario Historical Society Papers and Records* 17 (1919) 75.

[10] Winks, *Blacks in Canada* 6-7. For more on the sale of slaves in New France see William R. Riddell, "Notes on the Slave in Nouvelle-France," *Journal of Negro History* 3 (1923): 316-330.

[11] Winks, *Blacks in Canada*, 10.

[12] "Important Events in Canadian Black History," http://www.niica.on.ca/csonan/BlackEvents.aspx (accessed on September 2, 2006).

[13] Winks, *Blacks in Canada*, 9.

[14] By the 1770s there were an estimated 350,000 enslaved Africans in the North American colonies and approximately 75% were in the Carolinas, Virginia and Georgia http://collections.ic.gc.ca/blackloyalists/story/revolution/slavery.htm (accessed on 4 September 2006).

[15] Doris Calder, *All our Born Days: A Lively History of New Brunswick's Kingdom Peninsula* (New Brunswick: Percheron Press, 1984), 57.

[16] For more on the maroons see Alvin Thompson, *Flight to Freedom: African Runaways and Maroons in the Americas*, (Jamaica: University of the West Indies Press, 2006).

[17] "Story of Deportation of Negroes from Nova Scotia to Sierra Leone," Read by Ex-Governor Archibald, in *Collections of the Nova Scotia Historical Society for the Years 1889-91* (Halifax: Herald Publishing Company, 1891), 151.

[18] "Deportation of Negroes from Nova Scotia to Sierra Leone" 153.

[19] James Lockett, "The Deportation of the Maroons of Trelawny Town to Nova Scotia, Then Back to Africa," *Journal of Black Studies* 30 (1999): 7.

[20] See Tulloch 72-80. Also J.W. St. G. Walker, "On the Other Side of Jordan: The Record of Canada's Black Pioneers 1837-1865," unpublished paper, Canadian Historical Association Annual Meeting, London, Ontario, 1978. See also Ernest Green, "Upper Canada's Black Defenders," *Ontario Historical Society: Papers and Records* 25 (1931): 365-391. Fred C. Hamil, "Fugitive Slaves in Western Canada Prior to 1850," *Detroit Historical Society Bulletin* 2 (1945): 1-4. Hamilton J. Cleland, "Slavery in Canada," *Magazine of American History* 25 (1891): 233-238.

[21] See Phyllis Blakeley, "Boston King, A Negro Loyalist who sought refuge in Nova Scotia," *Dalhousie Review* 3 (1968): 351.

[22] *Telegraph-Journal*, October 4, 1980.

[23] John Grant, "Black Immigrants into Nova Scotia, 1776-1815," *Journal of Negro History* 3 (1973): 255. "The Black Nova Scotian odyssey: a chronology," *Race and Class* 40 (1998): 80.

[24] James W. St. G. Walker, *Black Identity in Nova Scotia: Community and Institutions in Historical Perspectives* (Dartmouth: Black Cultural Centre of Nova Scotia, 1985), 9.

[25] "Black Nova Scotian odyssey," 80.

[26] Ken Alexander and Avis Glaze, *Towards Freedom- The African Canadian Experience* (Toronto: Umbrella Press, 1996), 64.

[27] For instance see Grant, "Black Immigrants" 254. Grant, *Nova Scotians*, 8.

[28] Barry Cahill, "Stephen Blucke: The Perils of Being a "White Negro" in Loyalist Nova Scotia," *Nova Scotia Historical Review* 11 (1991): 129.

[29] G.C. Hormster to Captain Barrie, 1 June 1814. Adm. 1/507.

[30] Wayne Kelly, "Black Troops to Keep an Intelligent People in Awe!: The Coloured Companies of the Upper Canada Militia, 1837-1850" (MA thesis, York University, 1996).

[31] William R. Riddell, "Some references to Negroes in Upper Canada," *Ontario History* 22 (1925): 145.

[32] See Jerome Teelucksingh, "Family History of Early Blacks in Upper Canada," *Families* 38.4 (1999): 233.

[33] *Kitchener Waterloo Record*, July 17, 1997.

[34] *Galt Reporter*, December 10, 1858.

[35] *Guelph Mercury*, February 10, 1997. See also *Waterloo County Times*, Spring 1997.

[36] *Kitchener Waterloo Record*, December 1, 1990.

[37] *Kitchener Waterloo Record*, July 20, 1979.

[38] *Waterloo Historical Society*, 49 (1961): 47.

[39] Winks, "Negroes in the Maritimes," 456.

[40] *The Gazette*, January 25, 1997.

[41] "North Star of Freedom? African-Americans in Canada in the Days of the Underground Railroad," http://www.duke.edu/~mahealey/black_canada.htm (accessed October 4, 2006).

[42] "The Underground Railroad,"

---

http://www.blackhistoricalmuseum.com/undergroundrr.htm (accessed October 4, 2006).

[43] Charles Blockson, "Escape from Slavery: The Underground Railroad," *National Geographic* (1984): 39.

[44] H.H. Spencer, "To Nestle in the Mane of the British Lion: A History of Canadian Black Education, 1820-1870" (PhD diss., Northwestern University, 1970), 25. Also Fred Landon, "Fugitive Slaves in London before 1860," *London and Middlesex Historical Society Transactions* 10 (1919): 32-33.

[45] Landon, "Freeing the Slave," 76.

[46] Alexander and Glaze 59.

[47] Cheryl MacDonald, "Mary Ann Shadd in Canada: Last Stop on the Underground Railroad," *Beaver* (1990): 33. See also entry "Underground Railroad" in Peter Hinks and John McKivigan eds. *Encyclopedia of Antislavery and Abolition* vol. 2 (Connecticut: Greenwood Press, 2007), 692-694.

[48] Charles Blockson, *The Underground Railroad: Dramatic Firsthand Accounts of Daring Escapes to Freedom* (New York: Berkley Books, 1994), 207.

[49] Sharon Roger, "'Slaves No More': A Study of the Buxton Settlement, Upper Canada 1849-1861" (PhD diss., State University of New York at Buffalo, 1995), 27.

[50] Pease and Pease 62-63.

[51] Wayne Kelly, "Inside Uncle Tom's Cabin," *Heritage Matters* (2005): 2. Also "Uncle Tom's Cabin (1852)" in *Encyclopedia of Antislavery*, 691-692.

[52] Alexander and Glaze 58. The coloured population in Montreal had increased by 1860 and this was attributed to more persons utilising the Underground Railroad. This Black community in Montreal was described as being "sober, industrious and respectable" *Montreal Witness* April 18, 1860.

[53] "North Star of Freedom? African-Americans in Canada in the Days of the Underground Railroad," http://www.duke.edu/~mahealey/black_canada.htm (accessed October 4, 2006).

[54] Blockson, "Escape from Slavery," 9.

[55] Spencer 45. See *Voice of the Fugitive* November 5, 1851. Also *Annual Report*, American Anti-Slavery Society 1860, 48-49.

[56] See *Kent Advertiser*, October 17, 1850.

[57] See "History of Negro migration" Abbott Papers, Baldwin Room, Metropolitan Library, Toronto.

[58] Fred Landon, "The Anti-Slavery Society of Canada," *Journal of Negro History* 4 (1919):126. However, between 1861 and 1871 Methodists and Baptists in Chatham experienced an increase in Black membership. In 1871, the Methodists and Baptists recorded increases of 67% and 20% respectively. Walton 205.

[59] Annual Report of the American and Foreign Anti-Slavery Society presented at New York May 6, 1851, 31

[60] Jonathan Walton, "Blacks in Buxton and Chatham 1830-1890: Did the 49th Parallel make a difference?" (PhD diss., Princeton University, 1979), 276.

[61] See Jacque Voegeli, *Free But Not Equal* (Chicago: University of Chicago Press, 1967), 2.

[62] This Act meant the repeal of the Missouri Compromise (1820) that banned slavery from the land north of 36 degrees 30 minutes. It also allowed settlers in these new regions to decide if slavery should exist.

[63] *Elora Backwoodsman*, February 24, 1853.

[64] There were 5,489 fugitives in Canada in 1848. "Mission to the Free Coloured Population in Canada," 4 (1854) in *Colonial Church and School Society Annual Reports* 1851-1856. The 1851 census seems to have under-represented the total Black population in Upper Canada as 4,669. *Canada Census* 1851, vol.1, 317.This problem of misrepresenting the coloured population also occurred in the 1861 census because refugees fearfully avoided the census. Roger 29. First Annual Report presented to the Anti-Slavery Society of Canada 24 March 1852, 17. For difficulties in accurately presenting figures for the Black population in Canada see Winks, *Blacks in Canada*, 484-496.

[65] "The Underground Railroad."

[66] "History of Negro Migration to Canada" Abbott Papers, Baldwin Room, Metropolitan Library, Toronto.

[67] *Kent Advertiser*, October 17, 1850.

[68] Fred Landon, "Negro Migration to Canada after the passing of the Fugitive Slave Act," *Journal of Negro History* 5 (1920): 22. For more on the debate regarding population size see Blockson, *Underground Railroad*, 262.

[69] Table 1 "Negro Population of Toronto, Ontario and Canada 1851-1911" in Daniel Hill, "Negroes in Toronto: A Sociological Study of a Minority Group" (PhD diss., University of Toronto 1960), 35.

[70] *Voice of the Fugitive*, May 1851.

[71] *The Christian Reformer*, February 1861.

[72] *Evening Times-Globe*, August 5, 1992.

[73] Donald H. Clairmont and Dennis William Magill, *Nova Scotian Blacks: An Historical and Structural Overview* (Halifax: Institute of Public Affairs, Dalhousie University, 1970).

[74] Robin Winks, "Negroes in the Maritimes: An Introductory Survey," *Dalhousie Review* 48 (1968-69): 455.

CHAPTER TWO

SLAVERY IN THE UNITED STATES: SINNER OR SAVIOUR?

> Slaves, obey your earthly masters with respect and fear, and with sincerity of heart, just as you would obey Christ. Obey them not only to win their favor when their eye is on you, but like slaves of Christ, doing the will of God from your heart. ...And masters, treat your slaves in the same way. Do not threaten them, since you know that he who is both their Master and yours is in heaven, and there is favoritism with him. (Ephesians 6: 5-7, 9).

Pro-slavery ministers frequently cited this verse from the New Testament in the debate that the enslaved should be obedient to their masters. The overwhelming majority of churches in the United States failed to be outspoken critics of slavery. The wavering and indecision on the issue of slavery's abolition was indicative of racism and bigotry in Christianity during the nineteenth century in the United States. Some of the clergy selectively used Bible passages to justify slavery's existence. Additionally, there was the identification of Blacks as the cursed descendants of Ham or Cain, two historical figures in the Old Testament. Other arguments were that the servitude enforced in the Old Testament was proof that slavery was legitimised in the Bible.

Among the hallmarks of Protestantism was its personal responsibility, encouragement of social and civil virtues, and emphasis on free enquiry. In the early 1830s, the clergy tended to avoid the hotly debated issue of slavery and abolitionism. Nonetheless, the anti-slavery agitation contributed to irreparable schisms in several Protestant denominations. The moral ability and individual will given by God to each person was one of the beliefs of evangelicalism. Thus, it was sometimes argued that slavery deprived Blacks of these qualities and also salvation.[1]

For almost half a century after the War of 1812, there was the gradual emergence of two unique and separate cultures in North and South. In the South there was specialisation in the cotton industry which led to the pattern of "domesticating slavery."[2] This included Christianisation, corporate communalism and rejection of abstract rights. Meanwhile the

North developed an internal economy which was diversified. The creation of an anti-ecclesiastical and non-intellectual tradition in antebellum South was due to the influence of a frontier White underclass. Thus, the emergence of a religiously-flavoured political attitude was a result of the defense of slavery by Southern churches.[3]

A major phase in the abolition campaign occurred in December 1833 in Philadelphia when reformers from New York, the Quakers and New England Garrisonians convened and founded the American Anti-Slavery Society. A major difference between the anti-slavery movement in the pre-1830s and the abolitionist movement of the 1830s was the latter's urgent demand for an unconditional and immediate end of slavery. This demand arose from the acceptance that slaveholding was "a sin– always, everywhere, and only a sin."[4] Abolitionists in the post-1830s felt that the clergy and non-slaveholders needed to be forthright in their denunciation of slavery as a sin. Additionally, some abolitionists argued that the Bible obligated sinners to immediately end their wrong-doings.

However, church leaders believed this was too radical a step and instead advocated for a process of gradual emancipation including preparation of the enslaved for freedom and compensation to their masters.[5] One of the underlying reasons that abolitionists sought support from Protestant churches was because of the strong religious orientation of anti-slavery leaders. For instance, in 1838 in Philadelphia, pro-abolitionist evangelical churches formed the Church Union Anti-Slavery Society. The primary purpose of this proactive group was to remove the conservative influence of the clergy within their denominations.

Abolitionists were critical that clergymen in the South publicly defended slavery. The abolitionists publicly used the idea of slavery as a "national sin" to condemn residents in non-slaveholding states as guilty. This did not have the desired effect and it was apparent that the clergy was fearful of adopting a position on slavery which would contribute to a declining church membership. The abolitionists openly criticised Northern churches for having "Negro Pews" that separated Blacks from Whites. Undoubtedly, the abolitionists could not tolerate this segregation and delays in the transformation of denominational churches into anti-slavery voices. Differences in morality, theology and church policy among the Protestants served as major challenges to the abolitionists. Nevertheless, it was primarily due to irreconcilable differences over church practice and disagreements with the New England ministers that many Garrisonian abolitionists became anti-clerical and departed their congregations.

In the United States, the pro-slavery churches and the distorted interpretation of the Bible which supported slavery were painful reminders of the urgent need for independence of the Black churches in Upper Canada. For instance, in 1857, George Armstrong, a Protestant theologian, produced a treatise "The Christian Doctrine of Slavery" in which he argued that slavery's "essential" form did not constitute a sin or moral wrongdoing.[6] Similarly, in Missouri, there was a theologian who condemned the unethical aspect of slavery but, "... apologized for slaveholders and endeavored to rationalize their failure to free their slaves."[7]

The necessity of slavery for the continued prosperity of the cotton industry in the South and the entrenched racial prejudices served to circumvent and easily overcome anti-slavery feelings. It seemed that the churches lacked a genuine humanitarian outlook and brotherly compassion for enslaved human beings. Furthermore, the refusal and delay of the major Protestant denominations in the United States to publicly declare their opposition to slavery led to a steady exodus of the enslaved and free Blacks to Canada. John Ysursa supported the contention that that the factor of religion needed to be considered in understanding the causes of the Civil War.[8] The clergy in the South sought to define the moral aspects of political issues such as slavery. This led to the sectional conflict with religious connotations.[9]

Prominent Blacks as Frederick Douglass believed the Civil War was a religious war for Black freedom.[10] In 1852 Douglass vociferously condemned the hypocrisy in the United States, "The existence of slavery in this country brands your republicanism as a sham, your humanity as a base pretense and your Christianity as a lie."[11] Similar men as William Lloyd Garrison, a prominent antislavery agitator, dedicated their lives to demanding better treatment for the Blacks.[12] Some anti-slavery sympathisers in the North viewed the Civil War as the end of slavery and onset of racial equality.

Divisions among the Methodists

In 1774 John Wesley, the founder of Methodism, published a controversial pamphlet entitled *Thoughts on Slavery* which convincingly argued that Christian mercy and natural justice were incompatible with slavery. American Methodists genuinely believed that the abolition of slavery would result in the "moral transformation of the slave" and that the United States society could be drastically improved, "One aspect of the abolitionist controversy in the church was the search for a solution which was in harmony with what was thought to be the proper function of Methodism in American society."[13] This was similar to the initial goals of

Christianity, with its evangelical message, to redeem humanity rather than attempt to reconstruct society.

Some Methodists sought to convince slaveholders that promoting the belief in a better life after death as a reward for the righteous would make better enslaved Blacks. The underlying intention of this philosophy was to ensure the enslaved, in the hope of a future heavenly goal, would be diligent and subservient. Rev. James O. Andrew, a missionary among the enslaved noted, "Nothing is better calculated to render man satisfied with his destiny in this world, than a conviction its hardships and trials are as transitory as its honors and enjoyments...."[14] Indeed, conservative Methodists were concerned about the spiritual bondage of the enslaved and believed in the basic humanity of the Blacks. There were also concerns that the rebelliousness of the enslaved would be fostered by religious instruction. Among Methodists their stance on slavery stemmed from the belief that man was a moral and responsible individual. They believed a vital component of human nature was the freedom of will.

Early efforts of the Methodists sought to reduce an association of slavery with their denomination. In 1780, at the Annual Conference of the Methodists, the members declared slavery was, "contrary to the laws of God, man, and nature, and hurtful to society; contrary to the dictates of conscience and religion."[15] Furthermore, travelling preachers who possessed enslaved persons were requested to grant them freedom. Unfortunately, there was not a consensus to implement these anti-slavery principles. In early May 1785, the rules on slavery were suspended at both the Virginia and Baltimore Conferences. An official declaration of the Methodists had evolved by 1820 with a ban on the purchase or sale of children, men and women, which would lead to their enslavement.[16] In 1824 there was a provision in the rules of the Methodist Church for the religious instruction of the enslaved.[17] This had some impact on the number of enslaved converts. During the 1820s, there was an increase in the number of Whites and the enslaved who were attracted to Methodism in Georgia.[18] The challenges encountered by the Methodist Church demonstrated the extent in which the slavery proved to be a controversial issue.

During 1836-1840, there was widespread anti-slavery feeling among Methodists in New York and New England. This sentiment of abolitionism was a cause of concern at the General Conference of 1840 in which Southern Methodists united with conservative Northern Methodists to defeat measures which abolitionists believed favoured slavery. At the Conference, rules were adopted which prevented Blacks from testifying in Southern church trials. In protest, Methodist abolitionists organised anti-slavery conventions and founded the American Wesleyan Anti-Slavery Society in October 1840. In the early decades of the nineteenth century, Rev. Willbur Fisk, a Methodist minister and educator, was a strong advocate for African colonisation as a possible panacea for American slavery.[19] Edward Crowther, in his doctoral dissertation, contended that Protestants in the South felt that slavery was sanctioned by the Bible and the institution influenced Southern life. Due to this different attitude during the 1830s and 1840s, Southern Baptists and Methodists broke ties with their Northern compatriots and established separate churches.[20]

There was a major schism as a new branch of Methodism was formed which attracted anti-slavery Methodists. The first meeting of the Wesleyan Connection was held in 1841 under the leadership of abolitionists such as Orange Scott and La Roy Sunderland. The Wesleyan Connection with its 6,000 members was reorganised in 1843 and had a vibrant membership of 15,000 by 1845. The Methodists were acutely aware that if they did not openly denounce slavery they would continue losing members to the Wesleyan Connection in New England.

A further setback of the Methodist Church occurred in January 1844 when their denomination's leader, Bishop James O. Andrew, became embroiled in a controversy. This arose as a result of his marriage to a widow who owned enslaved persons. The issue was raised at the General Conference of 1844 but Andrew refused to resign. He was neither expelled nor faced disciplinary action but simply requested to cease his duties until the enslaved were freed. Not surprisingly, the incident of 1844 did not change the attitude and policy of the Methodist Church. Northern Methodist conservatives were not willing to implement official policy changes which would result in a loss of membership to the South.[21] Furthermore, Methodist conservatives believed that the ideal role of the Church should be as a peacemaker in the acrimonious debate over slavery.[22]

Prior to the 1830s, Blacks in Mississippi received equal treatment in the Presbyterian, Baptist and Methodist churches. After 1830, with an increase in holders of enslaved persons in the congregations and more wealthy members in the churches, this posed a moral dilemma for these churches. However, most White leaders continued to defend religious freedom of the enslaved and regularly opposed slavery.[23] Subsequently, there was an increase in the Black membership in these churches.

In the post-slavery era, the newly freed Blacks were being approached by missionaries from the various Methodist denominations- British Methodist Episcopal, Colored Methodist Episcopal, African Methodist Episcopal Zion, African Methodist Episcopal and Methodist Episcopal

Church, South. It was a dilemma for the ex-enslaved to choose one of these denominations which had different meanings of freedom. A "Gospel of Freedom" promising a new era was being promoted by both African Methodist denominations.[24]

Baptists, Lutherans, Congregationalists and Unitarians

The Baptists lacked a central structure of church government and thus there was no official policy on the issue of slavery. As a result of the lack of structure, anti-slavery groups encountered problems in convincing Northern Baptists that they were committing a wrong in their continued association with slaveholding Southern Baptists. In the early nineteenth century, the Kentucky and Midwestern Baptists had such anti-slavery associations as the Friends of Humanity. However, there was a belief even among anti-slavery Baptists the church had no power against the institution of slavery.[25] In the late eighteenth and early nineteenth centuries, Rev. John Leland, a Separate Baptist evangelist, was against slavery. He advocated separation of church and state.[26]

In 1835, slavery was declared a sin at the Free Will Baptists' General Conference and two years later, the denomination pledged support for the forthright abolitionist principles of the American Anti-Slavery Society. Some of the abolitionists who made lecture tours on behalf of the American Anti-Slavery Society were Baptist preachers as Elon Galusha, Cyrus P. Grosvenor and Nathaniel Colver. In an effort to prevent a loss in membership, the Baptist General Tract Society requested its workers to promise that they would not be involved in the divisive slavery debate.

The Texas Baptists welcomed the enslaved into their congregations and believed these oppressed peoples were children of God and worthy of salvation and religious teaching. It was paradoxical that these Baptists, who claimed to be religious, owned enslaved persons. In the post-Civil War era, it was inevitable that Black Baptists in Texas would withdraw from White-dominated churches and form separate churches.[27] There were similar features between the Texas Baptists and the Moravian Church (Renewed Unity of Brethren) in North Carolina who began their mission in 1753. A few Moravians possessed enslaved persons and because it was not extensive, many of the enslaved joined the Moravian Church.[28]

It would be erroneous to believe that in the United States all the churches belonging to a particular Christian denomination were either pro-slavery or abolitionist. Certain denominations as the Baptists had some churches that strongly condemned slavery whilst other Baptist congregations were pro-slavery. For example, the Baptist churches in the lower

Mississippi Valley had mixed reactions toward slavery. This was a result of cotton's profitability and its need for enslaved labour.

As a result of theological disputes, Unitarianism and Congregationalism emerged from New England as separate sects. Both churches had very few members in the South. By financial support to colonisation schemes, they displayed their prejudices against free Blacks in the North, "While many individual Congregationalists and Unitarians joined antislavery societies in the 1830s, the figures of authority in these predominantly northern churches resisted abolitionist appeals."[29] New Englanders of both denominations hoped that the disruption of state and church would be avoided by amelioration and colonisation.

Even though the Congregationalists projected an anti-slavery view, before 1860 they were not fully pro-abolition. A strong stance in churches, against owners of enslaved people was taken at anti-slavery conventions in Pennsylvania and Ohio in 1851 and 1855. These meetings were sponsored by the Free Presbyterians and Congregationalists from Oberlin College in Ohio.

In January 1835, the American Union for the Relief and Improvement of the Colored Race was founded by a group of concerned Congregationalists and Unitarian clergy. The philosophy of the group was supportive of the fraternal merging of abolition and colonisation programs. Williams E. Channing, an outspoken Unitarian, acknowledged slavery as being an evil system. However, he believed that the action of churches in condemning and banning members with enslaved persons was "counterproductive."[30]

Interestingly, the Roman Catholics and Lutherans sought to avoid religious discussions or passage of church legislation pertaining to slavery. The Roman Catholics did not tolerate racial discrimination yet they accepted those members, owning the enslaved, in their congregations. These liturgical denominations only expelled heretics and did not conform to the demands by abolitionists to reject slaveholders from their membership.

The Franckean Synod of Lutherans in New York enforced non-slaveholding as a test for membership in their congregation. However, friction developed between this group and the main Lutheran body which resulted in the latter deciding to secede.[31] The governing American Lutheran bodies refused to address the issue of slavery which they considered was a secular matter not to be discussed among the religious bodies.

Presbyterians: A Divided Church

During the 1790s there were vaguely worded proclamations by the Presbyterian Church which supported emancipation of the enslaved. In 1818, the Presbyterian General Assembly declared, "The voluntary enslaving of one part of the human race by another, as a gross violation of the most precious and sacred rights of human nature, as utterly inconsistent with the law of God...."[32] However, this resolution was described by critics as possessing "no teeth in terms of discipline."[33] Despite branding slavery as an evil system, the Presbyterian Church continued to allow its lay members and clergy to possess enslaved persons. The hypocrisy was obvious as the Presbyterians tolerated slavery in practice but opposed it in theory.

In 1837, there was a major schism in the Presbyterian Church which arose due to the debate over slavery. Four Northern Presbyterian synods were expelled as a result of their public denunciation of slavery. The reasons given by the General Assembly in 1837 was that the four synods had cooperated with liberal Congregationalists and secondly, they had adopted revivalistic preaching styles which contradicted traditional Calvinism.[34]

Alvan Stewart, an abolitionist, informed the Presbyterian National Assembly that it was "moral cowardice" of the church not to declare slavery as sinful. He further emphasised the danger of apathy, "silence soon becomes acquiescence, which is soon apology, which is soon defence, which is soon vindication."[35] Another member of the Presbyterian family had taken steps to end the oppressive labour system. In 1837, the American Anti-Slavery Society acknowledged the role of the Scottish Presbyterians in ending their support of colonisation schemes and also implementing anti-slavery doctrines.[36] South Carolina Presbyterians supported religious instruction of the enslaved. These Presbyterians felt this was vital for the salvation of both the enslaved and their masters.[37]

The more orthodox and larger "Old School" Presbyterians displayed questionable anti-slavery sentiments. Dissident Old School Presbyterians held denominational anti-slavery conventions in 1842 and 1845. The abolitionists praised these efforts but the conservatism of Presbyterians was evident at the General Assembly in 1845. The governing body of the Old School condemned the evils of slavery but stated that the Bible did not prevent slaveholders from receiving communion. Abolitionists pressured the Presbyterian Church to make a public statement against slavery. Finally, at the General Assembly in 1846, the "New School" (or theologically more evangelistic) Presbyterians acknowledged the oppressive slavery system and declared it unfair "by general and promiscious (sic) condemnation" to believe that all slaveholders be debarred from membership and deemed as sinful. In a similar manner, the Northern Methodists and Baptists acknowledged slavery as evil but not a sin.

The factionalism among the Presbyterians continued. The Free Presbyterians were formed as an option for Presbyterians who felt the churches were corrupt. This splinter group had forbidden communion with churches that had members who owned enslaved persons. Free Presbyterians even refused to offer communion to slavery-tolerating political candidates. In 1857, Old School Presbyterians curtailed communication with the Congregationalists. And, during the 1830s and 1840s, there were complaints from Western New School Presbyterians about their denomination's fellowship with owners of the enslaved. In an effort to increase its membership, the Free Presbyterians announced their willingness to merge with the anti-slavery sects of the Scottish Presbyterian Church. However, differences in doctrines prevented such a union. Indeed, Protestantism in the United States was neither monolithic nor homogeneous. The doctrinal discrepancies and sectionalism contributed to the conflicting and contradictory views on slavery. Undoubtedly, American churches were burdened with the dilemma of upholding their country as Christian, despite the existence of a cruel and inhumane system as slavery.

There was an inherent fear among churches in the United States that any major opposition to slavery would be a risky political venture with serious repercussions. The churches were not willing to risk losses in membership, repression by the United States government and condemnation by rival sects and other denominations. This was evident as churches refused to adopt and enforce strict measures to deter members owning the enslaved. Thus, hypocritical Protestants condemned slavery without any genuine desire for its abolition. It is obvious that churches were hesitant to disrupt the fairly stable church-state relations by challenging the political status quo. This fear of the government presented a major challenge for abolitionists as they were unable to obtain sufficient support from the smaller sects which banned slaveholders from their congregations. Some Protestant churches eased their conscience with the belief that slavery was a secular issue and should be dealt with by the governmental authorities. Ecclesiastical bodies deliberately and conveniently chose the easier and less controversial route of avoiding conflict and thus failed to align themselves to the abolitionists and become a united and outspoken voice for millions of oppressed Blacks.

The View from Canada

The Black churches in Canada distanced themselves from churches in the United States which were linked to slavery. During the 1850s, the Amherstburg Baptist Association continuously stressed the need to oppose the institution of slavery and in 1853 refused to recognise baptisms performed by ministers owning enslaved peoples.[38] In its anti-slavery resolutions in 1855, the Association appealed for prayers to focus on those suffering in slavery, "We also recommend the Churches composing this Association, to hold anti-slavery prayer meetings on the last Friday in every month, especially for the deliverance of the slaves from chains and all others that are oppressed by the deceptive plans of slaveholders."[39] The stance of the Black churches against slavery was the strongest indicator of their independence.

The *Provincial Freeman* was one newspaper that exposed Canadian churches which were linked to pro-slavery churches in the United States. Certain churches in Upper Canada were accused of distributing pro-slavery literature of churches from across the border. The Wesleyan Methodist Church in Canada had links to the pro-slavery Methodist Episcopal Church (North) in New York and received their publications. Likewise, the Free Presbyterian Church of Canada circulated literature from the pro-slavery Presbyterian Church of Chestnut Street, Philadelphia.[40] A similar accusation was levelled at the Regular Baptists of Canada and their fellowship with pro-slavery institutions such as the American and Foreign Bible Society of New York and the American Bible Union.[41] From mid-nineteenth century there were U.S. newspapers which reported on anti-slavery issues including the *Christian Recorder*, *Baptist Mission Herald* and *Star of Zion*.

After slavery ended, many of the freed Blacks chose a religion which was akin to their goals and values. Undoubtedly, their decision to join or remain in a Christian denomination was a milestone in their lives and was part of the re-defining of their identity as a freed people. It was considered as significant as adopting a new name.

Notes

[1] John McKivigan "Abolitionism and the American Churches, 1830-1865: A Study of Attitudes and Tactics" (PhD diss., Ohio State University, 1977), 19.

[2] See Marian Yeates, "Domesticating Slavery: Patterns of Cultural Rationalization in the Antebellum South, 1820-1860" (PhD diss., Indiana University, 1996).

[3] See Daryl White, "Denominationalism, Politics and Social Class: An Anthropological Analysis of Southern Protestantism" (PhD diss., University of Connecticut, 1985).

[4] *Anti-Slavery Record*, July 1, 1836.

[5] Nathan Bangs, *Emancipation: The Necessity and Means of Accomplishment Calmly Submitted to the Citizens of the United States* (New York: Lane and Scott, 1849), 14-17.

[6] See Archie C. Epps, "The Christian Doctrine of Slavery: A Theological Analysis," *Journal of Negro History* 46. 4 (1961): 243-249. See also Caroline L. Shanks, "The Biblical Anti-Slavery argument of the decade 1830-1840," *Journal of Negro History* 16 (1931): 132-157.

[7] W. Edward Farrison, "A Theologian's Missouri Compromise," *Journal of Negro History* 48 (1963): 35. There were some voices in the Southern states who resisted the ideology and practice of slavery. Two such men from Madison County, Kentucky (a slave state), were John Gregg Fee (1816-1901) (an abolitionist and Presbyterian minister) and Cassius M. Clay (1810-1903) both of whom were fearless and vocal opponents of slavery.

[8] See John Ysursa, "'A Leap of Faith': Religion and the Coming of the American Civil War" (PhD diss., University of California, 1996).

[9] See Mitchell Snay, "Gospel of Disunion: Religion and the Rise of Southern Separatism, 1830-1861" (PhD diss., Brandeis University, 1984).

[10] See David Blight, "Keeping the Faith in Jubilee: Frederick Douglass and the Meaning of the Civil War" (PhD diss., University of Wisconsin-Madison, 1985).

[11] Frederick Douglass, "What to the Slave is the Fourth of July?" Speech given in Rochester, New York July 5, 1852. See also Frederick Douglass, "Reception Speech" edited by Arthur L. Smith and Stephen Robbs eds., *The Voice of Black Rhetoric: Selections*, 31-45 (Boston: Allyn and Bacon, 1971).

[12] See Bruce Rogers, "The Prophetic tradition in Nineteenth Century America: William Lloyd Garrison and Frederick Douglass," (PhD diss., Drew University, 1992). See also Reverdy C. Ransom, "William Lloyd Garrison: A Centennial Oration," in *Voice of Black Rhetoric* 66-77.

[13] Milton B. Powell, "The Abolitionist Controversy in the Methodist Episcopal Church, 1840-1864" (PhD diss., State University of Iowa, 1963), 6.

[14] Susan Fickling, "Slave Conversion in South Carolina 1830-1860" (Columbia: University of South Carolina, 1924) *Bulletin of the University of South Carolina* 146 (1924): 12.

[15] Robert Emory, *History of the Discipline of the Methodist Church* (New York: G. Lane and C. Tippett, 1845): 14-15.

[16] *Doctrines and Discipline of the Methodist Episcopal Church* (New York: Methodist Publishing House, 1820), 78-79.

[17] Emory 279.

[18] Christopher Owen, "Sanctity, Slavery and Segregation: Methodists and Society in Nineteenth Century Georgia" (PhD diss., Emory University, 1991).

[19] See Douglas Williamson, "The Ecclesiastical Career of Willbur Fisk: Methodist Educator, Theologian Reformer, Controversialist" (PhD diss., Boston University, 1988).

[20] See Edward Crowther, "Southern Protestants, Slavery and Secession: A Study in Religious Ideology, 1830-1861" (PhD diss., Auburn University, 1986).

[21] Powell 142.

[22] Powell 159-160.

[23] See Randy Sparks, "A Mingled Yarn: Race and Religion in Mississippi, 1800-1876" (PhD diss., Rice University, 1988).

[24] Reginald Hildebrand, "Methodism and the Meaning of Freedom: Missions to Southern Blacks during the era of Emancipation and Reconstruction" (PhD diss., Princeton University, 1991).

[25] Robert G. Torbet, *A History of the Baptists* (Philadelphia: Jordon Press, 1950), 284-286.

[26] See John Creed, "John Leland, American Prophet of Religious Individualism" (PhD diss., Southwestern Baptist Theological Seminary, 1986).

[27] Richard Elam, "Behold the Fields: Texas Baptists and the Problem of Slavery" (PhD diss., University of North Texas, 1993).

[28] Jon Sensbach, "A Separate Canaan: The Making of an Afro-Moravian World in North Carolina, 1763-1856" (PhD diss., Duke University, 1991).

[29] McKivigan 77.

[30] McKivigan 86.

[31] See Douglas C. Stange, "Compassionate Mother to Her Poor Negro Slaves: The Lutheran Church and Negro Slavery in Early America," *Phylon* 29 (1968):150-151.

[32] Victor B. Howard, "The Anti-Slavery Movement in the Presbyterian Church, 1835-1861" (PhD diss., Ohio State University, 1961), 3.

[33] See John Christie and Dwight L. Dumond, *George Bourne and the Book Irreconcilable* (Philadelphia: Presbyterian Historical Society, 1969), 57-64.

[34] See James E. Johnson, "Charles G. Finney and a Theology of Revivalism," *Church History* 38 (1969): 338-358.

[35] Luther Marsh ed. *Writings and Speeches of Alvan Stewart on Slavery* (New York: A.B. Burdick, 1860), 187-188.

[36] By 1837 there were 225,000 Presbyterians in the United States. McKivigan 32.

[37] See Susan Ramey, "Salvation Black or White: Presbyterian Rationale and Protestant support for the Religious Instruction of Slaves in South Carolina" (PhD diss., University of Nevada, 1994).

[38] James K. Lewis, "Religious nature of the early Negro migration to Canada and the Amherstburg Baptist Association," *Ontario History* 58 (1966): 123.

[39] Lewis 123.

[40] *Provincial Freeman*, April 19, 1856; May 31, 1856; December 6, 1856. In Montreal and Toronto, the branches of the Young Men's Association refused to be

associated with any pro-slavery churches and slavery states. *Provincial Freeman* November 4, 1854; *Provincial Freeman* April 4, 1857. Certain individuals as Rev. S.B. Howe of New Brunswick used Biblical verses to argue that slavery was neither morally wrong nor sinful. *Provincial Freeman*, November 24, 1855.

[41] *Provincial Freeman*, December 6, 1856.

CHAPTER THREE

A CROWN OF THORNS:
THE CHURCH'S ROLE IN THE EDUCATION
OF BLACKS

I will give them a good education, which I could not do in the southern portion of the United States. True they were not slaves there, but I could not have given them any education.[1]

During the nineteenth century, education was increasingly influential in the lives of Blacks. Armed with literacy and knowledge, Blacks became responsible and respected leaders in their churches. Education was one of keys in unlocking the potential of Blacks and enabled them to successfully establish their own churches and thus be assimilated into Canadian society. Among Black communities the White Protestant churches were representative of the protective element of the Blacks. As a result of this emphasis on the importance of education by secular and religious institutions, Blacks seemed keen on seeking an education. By offering a mixture of religious and secular education the Protestant church hoped to create morally and intellectually sound individuals. Indeed, education, particularly in the mission schools, where differences between the races were minimised, was a crucial socialising factor. Education via the church provided Blacks with a golden opportunity to improve as they brought themselves closer to the ideal of virtuous citizens and thus better equipped for new social challenges.

One of the main factors contributing to the church's crucial educational role was the denial of education among Blacks in the United States. The restrictions of slave masters in the United States made Blacks more appreciative of the Protestant church's efforts in Canada. It was in the realm of education that religion left an indelible mark on the minds of intellectually-deprived Blacks. Their accounts proved that plantation masters in the United States had an underlying fear of Blacks and thus limited their access to education and religion. In St. Catharines, Canada, James Seward (originally from Maryland), recalled, "I was never sent to school, nor allowed to go to church. They were afraid we would have more sense than they."[2] The denial of education was present not only in the secular but in the religious realm as well. In 1855, James Sumler, originally from Norfolk, Virginia, recalled life under two masters who were Methodists:

> I was not sent to school-never. My first master and mistress gave me no religious instruction at all...My second master and mistress never gave me any instruction about God, and Christ, and the Bible: they used to object to my going to meetings.[3]

One of the factors contributing to varying levels of education among Blacks in Canada was the time spent in the middle states- Maryland, Kentucky and Virginia. The fugitives from these areas seemed to be better educated than their brethren in other states.[4] This was not surprising because there was a concerted effort to deny Blacks from receiving an education. Every Southern state except Maryland and Kentucky passed laws forbidding the teaching of reading and writing to the enslaved. In North Carolina it was a crime to distribute, to the enslaved, pamphlets and literature such as the Bible.[5] In 1864, a report on Blacks in Canada offered an explanation for the distinct differences in the rates of illiteracy, "those from the Free States had very little schooling in youth; those from the Slave States, none at all."[6] To a certain extent, geographical origin was important but there was also the factor of individual masters allowing religious or educational instruction. One illustration is Rev. Josiah Henson whose yearning for education began when he was thirteen years old in the United States. He purchased a spelling book with money obtained from selling his master's apples but on realising Henson's intention, the master flogged him and issued the threat, "remember if you meddle with a book again I'll knock your brains out."[7] Henson was traumatised and this experience had such a lasting impression that three decades later in Canada, he was able to muster the courage to continue reading. There some individual Protestants who disallowed Blacks from seeking an education. For example Charles Lucas, formerly owned by a Baptist minister in the United States, was denied schooling and religious instruction.[8]

The masters' exaggerated fear of educating Blacks was revealed in the recollections of the formerly enslaved. John Hunter, born in Maryland, was allowed by his first master to attend a school with White children. This was short-lived because upon the death of his master the new owner abruptly curtailed education believing that Hunter already knew too much.[9] Another illustration is Christopher Hamilton who spent his life in

St. Louis, Missouri. He vividly recalled his brief exposure to education, "I went to school a little, to a Sunday School, and learned to read, but was stopped-I suppose because I was learning too fast."[10] This religious and educational oppression endured by Blacks during slavery in the United States were pivotal factors in understanding their enthusiasm for the outreach programs in Canada. The attendance at the church's schools was one of the initial steps in formulating the importance of religion in their lives.

The ensuing social benefits that developed were not the main attraction to education. Among Blacks there was a desire to eliminate ignorance. Jason Silverman suggested that education was the medium to disprove racist beliefs by owners of the enslaved and other Whites who doubted the intelligence of Blacks.[11] Yet it also became apparent that the desire of Blacks to strive for education, was motivated by personal ambitions. Indeed, the majority of Blacks understood the value and importance of education as a vehicle to improve their status and condition.

After the abolition of slavery, returning free Blacks from Canada and the free Black population in the United States were hungry for education. Undoubtedly, the exposure to education in Canada would have proved to be the rationale for their demand for education in the United States. By 1865 there were 500,000 free Blacks in the United States and formerly enslaved persons comprised almost one-third of the population. Agencies such as the American Missionary Association (AMA), Freedmen's Bureau and the military, converted homes and churches into schools. They were also responsible for building night schools to educate adults. Thousands of teachers from the Northern United States travelled to the South to educate these free Blacks.[12] Many of the teachers taught at schools established by the Freedmen's Bureau.

Slavery's demise did not signal equality within the United States' education system. For instance, Blacks in New Orleans attended desegregated schools. However, at the end of the Reconstruction era, Whites restricted Blacks to a second-rate and inferior education in the state's primary and secondary schools.[13] Leland University, established during the Reconstruction era in New Orleans, served freed slaves and others desirous of education. The university was founded by a member of the American Baptist Free Mission Society and assisted by the American Baptist Home Mission Society.[14] In the post-slavery era, men such as Booker T. Washington boosted adult education through his efforts at Hampton Institute and Tuskegee Institute.[15] He is credited with shifting education from the classroom to the masses.

The Anglican Church and the SPG

The Anglican Church was actively involved in the education of fugitive Blacks. Rev. John Strachan of the Anglican Church had a similar vision, as Presbyterians, in training Blacks for the home mission. For instance, Strachan educated Peter Gallego, a Black, with the intention he would become a missionary and minister for Toronto's Blacks.[16] For the mission in Canada, the Anglican's Colonial Church and School Society appointed Rev. Marmaduke Martin Dillon, and three Blacks- sisters Sarah and Mary Titre and Richard Ballantine. In August 1854, the group arrived in Toronto. At its first meeting on 9 September 1854, Dillon explained that he intended to educate Canadian Blacks who would travel to Africa to save Black souls. This planned effort was not amicably received by the leading Black citizens in Toronto and the *Provincial Freeman* urged parents to boycott "the colored African school."[17] The underlying reasons could have been a low standard of schooling or an attempt to discourage segregated education.

Subsequently, Dillon, former Rector of Dominica in the British West Indies, was forced to move the mission to London, Canada West. This seemed a wise move as racially integrated schools existed in London. Dillon reported that the town school, opened in January 1855, had a satisfactory attendance of 61 children and reflected an interdenominational flavour of Anglicans, Baptists, Catholics and Methodists.[18] Also, he claimed that it was the first time that Black teachers were simultaneously teaching at both Black and White schools. After an inspection by a member of the Anti-Slavery Society, it was revealed that in London, the public schools had only 19 Black children whilst the Anglican school had 75 on its lists.[19]

Two schools were established by the Anglicans on an unused army quarters and one was referred to as the "Town school." A fee of 3 or 4 shillings was charged but by 1854 needy children were exempt from this fee. The subjects offered by the Anglican school in London included Spelling and Alphabet, Geography, Arithmetic, Scripture Reading, Needlework and Grammar.

In addition to being embroiled in controversies, Dillon's haughtiness and lack of diplomacy led to his abrupt departure from the mission in November 1855. Four year later, in 1859, a lack of proper leadership and funds resulted in the closure of the mission school at London. Shortly after this setback, the Colonial Church and School Society made an attempt to begin a school in Hamilton. However, financial troubles and prejudice plagued the brief appointments of Rev. Norman Fenn and later T.A.

Pinckney. The short-lived Hamilton mission was abandoned in 1861. The presence of the Protestant mission was also felt in relatively less populated areas, as in Colchester where the Colonial Church and School Society targeted the rural town for a school station.[20]

Other religious groups faithfully served Blacks in Canada. During the early years of the Black settlements White preachers and organisations as the Society for the Propagation of the Gospel (SPG) were keen in providing assistance and support to Blacks. Rev. Hiram Wilson, a White Congregationalist from Massachusetts, was a teacher in the British and American Manual Labor Institute at Dresden.[21] Whilst in the United States, Wilson was among the "Lane rebels" who disregarded the advice in 1834 of the Board of Trustees of the Lane Seminary in Cincinnati. They advised faculty and students not to be associated with antislavery efforts. In 1836 Wilson visited Canada and a year later addressed the Upper Canada Anti-Slavery Society. Almost 15 schools benefitted from money, Bibles and clothes from a Rochester-based group spearheaded by Wilson.[22] Undoubtedly, Wilson's stint in education in the United States contributed to the provision of quality education to Blacks.

Tolerance and Success: Mission and Sabbath Schools

The appreciation of education by Blacks is best illustrated in their consistent attendance records at the mission schools. One of the enduring legacies of the Presbyterian Church was their missionary efforts among Blacks in the Buxton mission.[23] Rev. William King, supported by the Presbytery of Toronto, spearheaded this religious effort. He believed that a church and school would satisfy the spiritual needs whilst eliminating ignorance and improving their moral and social conditions.[24] King also had his grounding in education with initial experience as rector of an educational institution in Louisiana overseeing the education of 200 male and female pupils. This administrative experience laid the foundation for his later novel educational work at Elgin.[25]

At the Buxton mission, King's insistence that, "the Bible would be read every day as a text book..." and the philosophy "the school would be conducted on religious principles"[26] were cornerstones on which the Buxton mission had been built. This supports the view that education was closely linked to religion and an underlying principle of the Protestant endeavor in Canada West. King's mission school with its challenging syllabus of Latin, Literature, History and Mathematics was undoubtedly equal and in some cases superior to that offered by other schools. Thus, by accepting Black children, the mission school demonstrated its genuine concern in assisting this oppressed segment of the population.

Church schools admitted children and adults of both races and some of the Black children in the Buxton mission were able to procure a college education whilst their illiterate and semi-literate parents were educated in literacy and business skills. This service of teaching strengthened the view that by 1850, Buxton had the most amount of literate Blacks than other Black communities in Canada and the United States.[27] This is in sharp contrast to the image of the Blacks, in common schools, who experienced intimidation and hardship.[28]

By 1856, the successful Buxton Mission school was partially supported by the Presbyterian Church of Canada and a decade later, King's report to the Elgin Association claimed that the mission school was self-supporting.[29] With a superb track record, it would have come as no surprise that in 1869 the exploits of the education experiment at Buxton had become legendary and there was one case in which a Black man attained tertiary education, "Already the schools have borne fruit. A few teachers trained at the schools, have been sent out to different parts of the province, where they are now usefully employed. Richard M. Johnson, one of the fugitives, is now studying in the University of Edinburgh as a medical missionary."[30] The success of King's missionary endeavours was reflected in the Presbyterian membership in Buxton.

Though the Buxton school might not have been wholly independent, it was a magnanimous attempt by King to portray the institution as capable of surviving without financial assistance from Whites.[31] Certainly King was aware of the shortcomings of existing Black settlements- Dawn and Wilberforce, but he was determined to make Buxton a success. He believed schools in Wilberforce and Dawn were failures because of a lack of proper organisation and insufficient financial assistance. King was optimistic that the young Blacks in Buxton would serve abroad as missionaries.[32] Through education men such as King proved that Blacks, if given an equal opportunity, "...are capable of making the highest attainments in knowledge, in morals, and in religion, and of reaching to the highest position in the social system."[33]

In December 1849, a Presbyterian church was organised with four members and 20 hearers and within eight years, the congregation could boast of 50 members and 200 hearers. By 1857, 100 pupils and eight teachers were enrolled in the Sabbath School and in May 1850, the Day School began with an initial number of 14 and eventually increased to a respectable total of 98 pupils.[34] The 1852 Report of the Anti-Slavery Society of Canada praised the Elgin settlement in the township of Raleigh, mainly because Black children were able to benefit from the school and fifty settlers willingly accepted the religious and moral instruction of King.[35] The enthusiastic response from Blacks at Buxton's churches and schools suggested that the educational experiment was on the road to success.

The attendance at the Sabbath schools was a visible indicator of the success of the mission schools in providing religious and secular education to the Blacks. The Sabbath School Report of the BME Conference in 1852 indicated the number of schools, scholars and teachers in their mission (see Table 3-1).

Table 3-1: Sabbath School Report

Place	Schools	Scholars	Teachers
St. Catharines	1	60	8
Toronto	1	50	6
Hamilton	1	48	2
Chatham	1	62	9
London	1	30	4

(Source: *Voice of the Fugitive* 26 August 1852).

During 1851-1852, the Sunday school classes of the AME Church in Toronto boasted a total of 50 pupils.[36] From 1856-1860, the Sabbath School of the St. Andrews Presbyterian Church at South Buxton recorded a promising average annual attendance of 76, whilst the years 1866-1870 produced a respectable annual figure of 83 pupils.[37] A similar success was recorded at the Wesleyan Methodist Sabbath School with 129 boys and 188 girls on the roll and an average attendance of 100 students.[38] The 1860-1870 reports of the Black Baptists revealed that Sabbath schools flourished in Hamilton, Sandwich, Amherstburg, Chatham and Dresden.[39]

Mary Ann Shadd, a well-known female educator of the era, taught at a school at Windsor during the 1840s. This institution catered for disadvantaged fugitives and its fees were four shillings per month. However, not all Blacks could afford this cost and the fee was reduced to three shillings. Continued financial difficulties forced her to temporarily close the school but it was opened when monetary relief was provided by the AMA.[40] The AMA also deserves credit for their invaluable contribution to education among Blacks. Rev. Hotchkiss, one of the AMA's missionaries rendered sterling service to the relatively small schools at Chatham, Mt. Pleasant and Puce.[41]

The Protestant church in early Canada was confident that its role in education would be jeopardised by inexperienced teachers. During the 1850s, Rev. Samuel Davis of the Baptist Church in Chatham served as an outstanding teacher at the school located at the 11th concession of Chatham Township.[42] Similarly, from 1861-1862, Rev. T. Hughes admirably served as missionary and schoolmaster at Dresden. Later in 1866, Hughes commented on the advantages of the laymen's leadership at the Dresden school, "Mr. Highgate continues to maintain the efficiency of our mission school which still remains the only one open to coloured children, in this district. Some four years there were even in the Black settlements three or four Separate Colored Schools carried on under the Common School Act of the Province, but they have all been closed...."[43] The constant emphasis on the value of education by such visiting men as Levi Coffin, a White abolitionist from the United States, emphasised the significance of the Sabbath and night schools for Blacks and their children.[44] The location of schools in close proximity to the Black settlement offered a golden opportunity for Blacks to improve their status in Canada.

In analysing the success of the mission schools, there is the tendency to believe that at the inter-racial schools, the Blacks would be judged differently and treated as being less privileged than Whites. However, there is no evidence proving that the standard of teaching and learning at these mission schools was inferior or different from that of White separate schools.[45] In fact by 1850, the Buxton School had earned such a reputation for teaching that some Whites sent their children to the institution.[46] The act of entrusting authority to Black laymen was a milestone in the stormy relationship between the two ethnic groups. It meant that some Whites had confidence in Blacks, whilst other Whites grudgingly acknowledged the abilities of Blacks. This was an important and vital phase as the White clergy was now able to seek assistance on church-related matters and spreading the Gospel to new missions in rural areas. The sharing of responsibilities was illustrated in 1851, when the Elgin Association reported that the Sabbath school was maintained by a superintendent and eight teachers.[47] Undoubtedly, this gradual transition of authority and responsibility to Black Protestant leaders in the churches and schools appealed to the relatively small Black population.

Coloured, Grammar and Common Schools:
Setbacks and Segregation

In Amherstburg in 1811, Mrs. L. Foster, a Black, sought admission for her children into the Common school but was rejected. The committee of school trustees coldly replied to Foster's husband, "The trustees are of the opinion that is inexpedient to alter the present arrangement of the different departments in as much as the colored department is sufficient for the wants of the colored people."[48] Amidst this segregation in the public education system, the Protestant mission schools carved a niche with their high quality of education and integrated classes and proved an attractive alternative to the common schools.

By the mid-1840s Upper Canada had approximately 97,000 pupils being taught in 2,610 schools and by 1860 there was an increase to 256,934 students. However, there is an absence of information as to the total number of Blacks attending these schools and the number of separate schools catering for their needs.[49] In terms of attendance, the Black population rivalled that of Whites in Canada West. In one survey in 1849, there was a reported increase in Common schools from 927 to 2,464 with an accompanying rise in attendance.[50] However, the shortcoming of the legislation was that it, "...effectively reinforced and legally entrenched a system of segregated schools for blacks in Canada West."[51] The passage of this Act meant that even if Black children attended the same school as Whites, the physical contact between the races would be limited as Blacks had to contend with either segregated benches or forced to attend at different times. Whites believed that the association of their children with Blacks would lead to a deterioration in their children's morals.[52] In the legal sense, separate schools for both ethnicities did not exist but the denial of education inevitably led to separate schools catering for Blacks.[53]

Interestingly, there was a concerted effort of the Protestant churches to use education as a tool to attract ambitious Blacks to its institutions. The creation of the mission schools was a direct response to the discrimination and difficulties experienced by Blacks in common and separate schools. There were optimistic signs at Dawn as the Sabbath and Bible classes were well-attended.[54] During the 1840s the demand for separate schools for Blacks intensified as they were excluded from common schools in Chatham. This prompted the American Baptist Mission, during 1843 to 1844, to allocate money for a teacher in Chatham. Despite this goodwill gesture the lone school was inadequate for the young Blacks and a separate common school was soon established.[55] In 1837 a separate school for Blacks in Brantford offered superior teaching instruction than the

White school.[56] The establishment of separate schools were a necessity for Blacks who were being denied an education in Canada.

In 1849, Shadd published a pamphlet entitled *Hints to the Coloured People of the North*. This publication was an appeal for Blacks to become independent, adopt the initiative in charting their destiny and discontinue the reliance on committees with lengthy delays in decision-making. Furthermore, Shadd was critical of Blacks who continuously begged philanthropic individuals and organisations. She refused to teach in segregated schools which were common in Upper Canada and thus did not renew her membership in the AME church.[57] Likewise, she did not support the existence of all-Black settlements such as the Dawn Settlement, and was a strong advocate for integration and assimilation into the Canadian society.

The issue of separate schools was not a major concern of government policy till the 1830s and almost two decades later, one of the debates in the Legislative Assembly over the Common School Act of 1850 sympathised with this disadvantaged segment of the population. One of the parliamentarians noted:

> These people are taxed for the support of Common schools as are others; yet are their children excluded from the schools. I have exerted all the power that I possessed, and employed all persuasion I could command; but the prejudices and feelings of people are stronger than the law.[58]

The institutionalisation of racism was embodied in the Act of 1850 which allowed for the creation of separate schools for Blacks.[59] The 9th section of the School Act attempted to rectify the problem by authorising the district councils to educate Blacks by creating separate schools. The Whites circumvented this by simply sending their children to separate schools, thus hastening the collapse of Common schools.[60] Though common schools generally provided sub-standard education, when compared to the United States, it seemed that Canada West had revolutionised its educational system:

> The common schools, though inferior to those of several of the states of the United States, are good. Coloured children are admitted to them in most places; and where a separate school is opened for them, it is as well provided by government with teachers and apparatus as the other schools are.[61]

By 1851 in Chatham, a distinct educational endeavour was underway as night schools for adults, Sabbath schools and day schools were in operation.[62] In 1842, in Colchester township, there were 3 separate schools for Blacks and by 1850 there were 4 schools serving the educational needs of 228 Blacks. Similarly, by 1857 in St. Catharines, the sole existing Black school had 3 pupils and one year later boasted 60 students.[63] Probably superior teaching attracted Blacks to this school. The separate school system for Blacks served a dual purpose as it fostered a spirit of independence and removed obstacles from the road for learning.

In November 1852, Dennis Hill, a Black from Dawn Mills in Canada West, pleaded with Egerton Ryerson to address the discrimination meted out by the trustees of school section No. 3 in the township of Camden in the County of Kent. Hill lamented:

> I have used every respectful effort in my power to have my son, eleven years of age, admitted into the above named school, but all to no purpose, they say that I am a black man and that it would be presumption as I see to me to contend for my son to go to school among white children, though I am among the largest tax payers in the said school system.[64]

This was evidence of the frustration that hundreds of Blacks encountered in a racist and élitist society. In the post-1853 period, the coercion of Blacks to pay taxes for schools that they were debarred from attending was deemed a criminal act.[65] The inability of the law to change the mentality of prejudiced Whites was evident from the closure of two schools- Saltfleet No. 3 and Grimsby No. 4 in which the teacher refused to teach Black children.[66] Blacks were fortunate that their request for separate schools was granted by the provincial government but prejudice in education continued to rear its ugly head as the educational inequities between schools for both ethnic groups widened. These separate schools were intended to preserve the assumption of equality and slowed the process of cultural assimilation.[67]

Despite evidence of the crucial value of education, there were obstacles for Blacks. The attendance of Blacks at church schools seemed to suggest a different quality of education was being offered. One assumption was that these mission schools catered for the slower rate of learning of Blacks. This would have resulted in a lowering of standards and adoption of different criteria when compared to White schools. This is illustrated in the Chatham Grammar School (established in 1855) which was devoid of Blacks because they were unable to pass the entrance exams.[68] Indeed, the Grammar schools had certain requirements for admission:

> In order for a pupil to be admitted to the grammar school he must be able to read intelligently and correctly any passage from any common reading book, to spell correctly the words of an ordinary sentence, to write a fair

hand, to work readily questions in the simple and compound rules of arithmetic....[69]

By 1856, during a visit to a separate coloured school at Sandwich there was evidence that a substandard education persisted, "The coloured teachers who present themselves are examined with a deal of "lenity" and some who cannot even spell, are placed in charge of the young."[70] Supportive of this view of an inferior education is Susan Houston and Allison Prentice who believed that though legislation prevented the collapse of Black education it, "condemned blacks to poorer schools with least qualified teachers."[71] Nevertheless, the majority of church schools, such as at Buxton, performed admirably and were judged a success by both Blacks and Whites.

In 1856, London and Chatham neglected Common schools because Blacks were in attendance and separate schools were established to serve Blacks.[72] Ryerson supported active separatism by 1859, and argued that trustees of schools could establish the most suitable school in their communities. The interpretation of Ryerson's advice, "...was to create local and separate Negro schools; while by law such schools were to be established only in response to requests from Negroes."[73] By 1862, London which had earlier gained prominence for its outward display of sympathy towards the Blacks, enacted legislation to separate its 50-80 Black pupils. By 1864 it was estimated that the average daily attendance of scholars in Black schools was 70%, not differing a great deal from attendance records at White schools.

The acts of segregation were not surprising because most Whites in such places as Chatham were deemed "hostile and racist."[74] Sinclair, a teacher at a public school in Chatham observed that when a White woman marries a Black, "The whites will have nothing to say to her, and her society is entirely with the blacks."[75] In 1856, Drew's observation held true for other Black settlements in Canada, "The prejudice against the African race here is very strongly marked...They sent their children at once into the public school. As these sat down the white children near them deserted the benches, and in a day or two, the white children were wholly withdrawn, leaving the schoolhouse to the teacher and his colored pupils."[76] Likewise, at Dresden, in the Dawn settlement, Whites and Blacks were reportedly prohibited from attending the same classes. The problem was further compounded as Dawn suffered from "religious sectarianism" and "black factionalism."[77] Likewise, schools at Hamilton and Colchester displayed sectarianism and prejudice in their education system.[78]

In 1862, one of the local schools in Chatham once boasted of 50 White pupils but due to the presence of Blacks, the attendance quickly dwindled to seven Blacks and two Whites.[79] Rev. William Troy, a Virginian serving the Baptist Church in Windsor, expressed his disappointment over this unjust system of segregation in the education system. In the outlying area of Simcoe, a similar situation occurred in the schools, "...during the past year the Children of your petitioners have been turned out of the Schools in Simcoe for the sole reason, that the (sic) differ in Colour from the great body of the other pupils."[80]

It became increasingly apparent that schools for Blacks were inferior, plagued by irregular attendance and staffed with incompetent teachers.[81] The prejudices existing in common and separate schools reduced the educational alternatives of Blacks but increased the likelihood of benefitting from education provided by the churches. Through education provided by the mission schools, Blacks were able to benefit from a sound education and became more appreciative of the churches' efforts. For example, in Chatham the coloured school was supported by the Free Mission Baptist Society and in Windsor, the coloured school was founded by the AMA. The integrating efforts of the mission schools benefitted an overwhelming majority of the Black students.

Using evidence of segregation in schools, Jason Silverman and Donna Gillie argued there was a correlation between the increase of the Black population and the subsequent rise in prejudice against the fugitives.[82] It can be argued that discrimination was not pervasive throughout the educational institutions in Canada West. There were instances when racially mixed classrooms in the public schools prevailed over the apparent norm of segregation. For instance, in Hamilton, public schools organised by the Church of England freely admitted Blacks into its integrated classes. Similarly, in Brantford, Galt and Toronto, both ethnic groups attended the same schools.[83] By 1840 in Amherstburg, James Dougal, a White layman, pioneered the establishment of a school which allowed both ethnicities to be educated in the same environment but this bold experiment was short-lived with a life span of six years.[84] Also, in 1843 the Governor-General was petitioned by Blacks in Hamilton seeking the right to public schooling.[85] Such pioneering experiments in integration proved that within the education system Blacks were being successfully assimilated.

Black Education in Nova Scotia, Prince Edward Island and New Brunswick

In Nova Scotia, the SPG played a crucial role in educating Blacks in New Brunswick and Nova Scotia from 1790 to 1850. In 1790, Bishop Charles Inglis of the SPG chose a Black, Thomas Brownspriggs, to serve as a teacher at a school with 23 Black children. However, Brownspriggs left this post after three years. More than two decades later, in 1813, a retired army official opened a school for Blacks, Indians and poor Whites in Halifax. Five years later, this school and the one in Tracadie were placed under the jurisdiction of schoolmasters appointed by the SPG.[86]

In Nova Scotia, separate schools also existed. In Preston, there was a school for Blacks which had a diligent Black teacher- Catherine Abernathy. This school was initiated by concerned White citizens of Preston and there were other similar schools which continued due to financial assistance by Whites.[87] By 1830 areas such as Digby, Halifax, Shelburne and Preston had schools for Blacks.[88] The education officials in the province did not express any serious concern to assist or improve education of Blacks. An amendment to the Education Act of 1836 allowed authorities to use part of a grant of £70 "…to establish schools for blacks even if common schools already existed."[89] A separate sum of £60 was allocated to the African School based in Halifax. Other schools in Canada benefitted from external assistance. In Nova Scotia, during the 1830s, there were Black schools existing in Preston, Hammonds Plains, Shelburne and Digby. These were supported by a British philanthropic society comprised of Whites.[90]

In Prince Edward Island and New Brunswick where the Black population was numerically smaller, most Black and White students attended the same schools. However, in Charlotte in Prince Edward Island, most of the Blacks attended a single school. Similarly, in Fredericton, New Brunswick, racist Whites contributed to Black children being illiterate and who were forced to seek separate educational institutions.[91] The provincial legislature in 1848 provided a financial grant for a day school, which enrolled 40 Blacks. It was located near Saint John at the "Coloured Settlement, Loch Lomond." Halifax's Legislative Assembly, in 1865, passed legislation which authorised the separation of White and Black schools. The passage of such discriminatory laws was due to the increasing Black population and concerns expressed by Whites.

Throughout Canada one of the factors aiding education's role among Blacks was the knowledge, experience and sincerity of some of the clergy. Furthermore, the fluidity between religion and education was not confined to any one denomination. Undoubtedly, the Protestant efforts among Blacks were not restricted to the ritual and theological concerns. Instead, education marched alongside religion seeking to eradicate years of social, cultural and economic deprivation and ignorance among the Blacks. The existence of both religious and secular subjects at mission schools was one of the hallmarks of education among Blacks in Canada.

The work of the Protestant Church in education assumes greater significance when one considers the intense discrimination within the school system. The relatively low levels of discrimination in the mission schools seemed a viable alternative for the Blacks in public schools. The services rendered by these Christian groups, churches and mission schools were essential in educating, shaping leaders and creating an environment favourable for assimilation in Upper Canada's society. Undoubtedly, the concerns and efforts of the White religious leaders in providing an education for the Blacks were to have a lasting effect. Blacks responded to this religious freedom by combining secular and religious education in their crusade of improving themselves.

Notes

[1] A Black citizen of St. Catharines informing Benjamin Drew of the opportunities for his children in Canada. Benjamin Drew, *A North Side View of Slavery* (Boston: John P. Jewett and Co., 1856), 86-87. Also Spencer 61-62.

[2] Drew 41.

[3] Drew 97.

[4] David Nitkin, "Negro Colonization as a Response to Racism: a Historical Geography of the Southwestern Ontario Experience, 1830-1860" (MA thesis, York University, 1973), 80.

[5] Stanley Elkins, *Slavery - A Problem in American Institutional and Intellectual Life* (Chicago: University of Chicago Press, 1976), 60.

[6] Samuel Gridley Howe, *The Refugees from Slavery. Report to the Freedmen's Inquiry Commission* (Boston, 1864), 77.

[7] Josiah Henson, *An Autobiography of Rev. Josiah Henson (Mrs. Harriet Beecher Stowe's "Uncle Tom" From 1789-1876* (London: Christian Age Office, 1876), 188-189.

[8] Drew 105. Lucas was resident in Toronto at the time of the interview.

[9] Drew 114. Hunter was at Toronto at the time of his interview.

[10] Drew 175.

[11] Jason Silverman, "Unwelcome Guests: American Fugitive Slaves in Canada 1830-1860" (PhD diss., University of Kentucky, 1981), 169.

[12] See Janice Stennette, "Teaching for the Freedmen's Bureau: Lynchburg, Virginia, 1865-1871" (PhD diss., University of Virginia, 1996).

[13] Donald Devore, "Race Relations and Community Development: The Education of Blacks in New Orleans, 1862-1960" (PhD diss., Louisiana State University and Agricultural and Mechanical College, 1989).

[14] Janice Johnson, "Leland University in New Orleans, 1870-115" (PhD diss., University of New Orleans, 1996).

[15] Virginia Denton, "Booker T. Washington and the Adult Education Movement, 1856-1915" (PhD diss., University of Southern Mississippi, 1988).

[16] John Strachan to Rev. A.M. Campbell April 28, 1840, 7. Rev. Strachan estimated the Black population in Toronto to be 500. *John Strachan Letterbook* Strachan Papers, Archives of Ontario (hereafter denoted as AO)

[17] *Provincial Freeman*, September 16, 1854.

[18] "Mission to the Free Coloured Population" Occasional Paper. no.2 December, 1854, 5-8.

[19] "Mission to the Free Coloured Population" Occasional Paper. no. 4. October 1855, 10. See also University of Western Ontario Archives, Huron College. Letter Book of the Rev. Marmaduke Martin Dillon, 1854-1856.

[20] Drew 369

[21] J.C. Hamilton, "The African in Canada," *Knox College Monthly* 11 (1889): 30.

[22] Winks, *Blacks in Canada*, 179.

[23] Also referred to as the Elgin Settlement it was located 17 miles southwest of Chatham.

[24] Minutes of the Synod of the Presbyterian Church of Canada, Toronto 1844-1852, 196, 254-255. Presbyterian Church Archives, Toronto (hereafter denoted as PCA), see also R.A Falconer, "Liberal Education in Canada," *Canadian Historical Review* 8 (1927): 99-118.

[25] Copy of Poster of Mathews Academy, Jackson, Louisiana. of which William King was Rector, 2 December 1841. PCA.

[26] *Autobiography of Rev. William King, written at intervals during the last three years of his life. January 6, 1892.* Typed copy at PCA. In the post-1870 period the emphasis on the Bible as a text in schools continued. In Dr. Abbott's address at the Sabbath School Anniversary at Chatham he advised, "the Bible as our infallible guide and rule of faith should be the groundwork of all religious instruction." Abbott Papers, Baldwin Room, Metropolitan Library, Toronto.

[27] Roger 409.

[28] Houston and Prentice 300.

[29] See A.M. Harris, *A Sketch of the Buxton Mission and Elgin Settlement, Raleigh, Canada West.* (Alabama, 1866), 7. The Buxton experiment was accepted as a success *Liberator* March 4, 1853.

[30] Rev. W.M. King and Robert Burns, *Fugitive Slaves in Canada, Elgin Settlement* (July, 1869) n.p.

[31] By the late 1850s, the Buxton settlement had three schools and four churches. The settlement, of more than 700 fugitive slaves and free Blacks, was mainly based on agriculture and there was a lumber mill and facility for brick-making.

Sharon Roger-Hepburn, "The Buxton Settlement: A Community Transformed by the Civil War and Emancipation," unpublished paper presented at the Great Lakes History Conference, Michigan, November 2003, 1.

[32] Walton 42. *Chatham Gleaner* December 5, 1848.

[33] Third Annual Report of the Elgin Settlement 1852 n.p AO. "...even those who advocate separate schools, promise that they shall be equal to white schools." Howe 78.

[34] Seventh Annual Report of the Buxton Mission presented at the meeting of Synod in Kingston, June 16, 1857, in Minutes of the Synod of the Presbyterian Church of Canada at its Session at Kingston, Canada West, 9-17 June 1857 (Toronto, 1857), 41. PCA.

[35] First Annual Report, Anti-Slavery Society 1852, 16.

[36] *Voice of the Fugitive*, July 10, 1852.

[37] Compiled from minutes of the Presbyterian Church Synod 1856-1860 and 1866-1870. P.C.A

[38] *St Catharines Constitutional*, March 21, 1867.

[39] A History of the Amherstburg Regular Missionary Baptist Association. Canadian Baptist Archives, McMaster Divinity College, Hamilton (hereafter denoted as CBA), 23.

[40] Shadd held the distinction of being the first female newspaper editor in North America.

[41] See Fifth Report of the American Missionary Association 1851, 32; Fifteenth Report of the American Missionary Association 1861, 29.

[42] "Biographies" McCurdy Papers, AO.

[43] "Mission to the Coloured Population" 9. *Annual Report Colonial Church and School Society*. 1866-1870, vol 3.

[44] See Levi Coffin, *Reminiscences of Levi Coffin* (New York: Arno Press, 1968). During the 1840s in the United States, Coffin and Charles Osborn formed the "Indiana Yearly Meeting of Anti-Slavery Friends" which expanded to more than 2,000 members.

[45] Lulu M. Johnson, "The Negro in Canada, Slave and Free" (MA thesis, State University of Iowa, 1930), 86.

[46] Walton 51. Also Spencer 40.

[47] Eighth Annual Report of the Directors of the Elgin Association, Presented at the Annual Meeting 2 September 1857.

[48] Carole Jensen, "History of the Negro Community in Essex County, 1850-1860" (MA thesis, University of Windsor, 1966), 25.

[49] Winks, "Negro School Segregation," 173-174.

[50] *Amherstburg Courier*, April 21, 1849.

[51] Jason H. Silverman and Donna J. Gillie, "The Pursuit of Knowledge Under Difficulties": Education and the Fugitive Slave in Canada," *Ontario History* 74 (1982): 100. See Egerton Ryerson, "Annual Report of the Normal, Model and Common Schools in Upper Canada for the Year 1852" *Sessional Papers of the Provincial Parliament of Canada Session* 1853 (Quebec, 1853).

[52] Spencer 112.

[53] Spencer 110-115.

[54] *Liberator*, March 1, 1850.

[55] *Chatham Gleaner*, November 11, 1845.

[56] Robin Winks, "Negro School Segregation in Ontario and Nova Scotia," *Canadian Historical Review* 50 (1959): 171.

[57] MacDonald 34. By 1852, Shadd had forged a close relationship with Rev. Samuel Ringgold Ward, an orator and Black minister who served a White congregation. Ward was the editor of the *Provincial Freeman*, but Shadd willingly undertook most of the workload as publisher, editor and subscription agent. In 1854, Shadd settled in Toronto, the province with the largest Black population. The public did not appreciate a woman being editor of a newspaper and she succumbed to public pressure and relinquished the position to a male editor at Chatham.

[58] The report of the Legislative Council was dated July 5, 1850. There was also mention that "not a single municipality in the County of Essex would establish a school for the education of their children" *Kent Advertiser*, July 18, 1850.

[59] With regard to the passage of the Act and its effect on schools in Upper Canada see *Amherstburg Courier*, January 5, 1850. See also *Globe and Mail*, March 13, 1964; Winks, "Negro School Segregation" 175. *Kent Advertiser*, July 18, 1850; *Amherstburg Courier and Western District Advertiser*, January 5, 1850.

[60] Houston and Prentice 152, 299.

[61] Howe 77.

[62] *Voice of the Fugitive*, September 10, 1851.

[63] Winks, "Negro School Segregation" 174, 176.

[64] Letter from Dennis Hill to Egerton Ryerson, November 22, 1852. Ryerson Papers, AO.

[65] Spencer 111.

[66] Prentice and Houston 152.

[67] Jean R. Burnet, "Ethnic Groups in Upper Canada" (MA thesis, University of Toronto, 1943), 32, 57. The Separate School Act was initially supposed to cater for the needs of the French Canadians outside of Quebec.

[68] Walton 78.

[69] *Windsor Herald*, August 25, 1855 cited in Spencer 85.

[70] Drew 341.

[71] Susan Houston and Allison Prentice, *Schooling and Scholars in Nineteenth Century Ontario* (Toronto: University of Toronto Press, 1988), 300.

[72] In 1851 Blacks comprised 17% of the population in Chatham and after a decade this figure increased to 28%. Houston and Prentice 298.

[73] Winks, "Negro School Segregation," 176. Ryerson to William Horton February 21, 1859. Ryerson to A.R. Green, March 10, 1859. Ryerson Papers, AO.

[74] Howard Law, "Self reliance is the true road to independence : ideology and ex-slaves in Buxton and Chatham," *Ontario History* 77 (1985): 104,114

[75] Howe 32.

[76] Drew 341-342.

[77] Winks, *Blacks in Canada*, 196.

[78] Drew 147, 235-236, 308,348, 368. See also Silverman and Gillie 98-101.

[79] *Provincial Freeman*, July 19, 1856; Winks, "Negro School Segregation," 177.

[80] Letter to 'Mr. Honourable' The Municipal Council of the County of Norfolk by coloured citizens of Simcoe County of Norfolk, December 17, 1850, Fred Landon Notes, University of Western Ontario.

[81] Winks, "Negro School Segregation," 177.

[82] Silverman and Gillie 106.

[83] Silverman and Gillie 148, 117. Also Winks, "Negro School Segregation," 171; Spencer 48; Drew 136.

[84] Roger 351-352. James Dougal was a Scottish Immigrant. Daniel Hill, *Freedom Seekers* (Agincourt: Book Society of Canada, 1981), 149

[85] Winks, "Negro School Segregation," 171. Drew 121.

[86] Winks, "Negro School Segregation,"168.

[87] Maureen Elgersman, *Unyielding Spirits: Black Women and Slavery in Early Canada and Jamaica* (New York: Garland Publishing, 1999), 149.

[88] Winks, "Negro School Segregation," 169.

[89] Ibid.

[90] Clairmont and Magill 22.

[91] Winks, "Negro School Segregation," 168-169.

CHAPTER FOUR

TRAINING OF DISCIPLES:
DEVELOPMENT OF BLACK LEADERSHIP

Teach slaves to be subject to their masters in everything, to try to please
them, not to talk back to them, and not to steal from them, but to show that
they can be fully trusted, so than in every way they will make the teaching
about God our Savior attractive (Titus 2: 9-10).

Most of the Blacks initially belonged to the Protestant faith, particularly
the Methodist and Baptist denominations.[1] Earnest Bell believed that the
Black preacher has been the spokesperson for United States Blacks. He
contended that the messages of the Black preacher, which were absorbed
by the enslaved and Whites, led to socio-political reforms.[2] Undoubtedly,
the influence of the Black preacher extended beyond the pulpit.

In a study of Essex County, in Canada West, from 1850 to 1860 it was
discovered that most of the Blacks were devout and guided by ministers of
the Sunday schools and churches.[3] During the process of integration and
assimilation into Canadian society, leaders arose within the Black
community who guided, provided inspiration and direction. Indeed, it
seemed that Blacks, "...wanted preachers who spoke to them in a language
and perhaps with an accent they might readily understand."[4] The nature of
Black leadership was limited, primarily due to a scarcity of experienced
leaders and scattering of the mission stations. It was necessary to share
resources which initially involved reliance upon visiting or temporary
spiritual leaders from the United States and other townships in Canada.
The separation of Black and White churches subsequently led to the
development of Black leaders and the inevitable transition from White to
Black leadership. It simply meant another step in the independence of
Black churches. This transfer of responsibility did not result in a major
modification of church organisation or preaching styles. During the
slavery era, the denial of leadership opportunities in the United States did
not seriously hamper the development of Black leaders in Canada. In the
United States, the degrading system of slavery stifled the leadership
potential of many Blacks. For example, Black ministers, in fear of being

whipped by masters, frequently stressed the importance of obedience of the enslaved.[5] Indeed, life in the United States was one in which discipline and obedience were enforced through violence. Blacks had to be respectful, peaceful and subservient to Whites. The Blacks dared not challenge or disrupt the status quo.

Inadequacy and Ignominy

A minority of the exodus of Blacks, to Canada, had some previous job experience be it tradesmen, servants in the master's house or overseers in the fields. Yet, it was a remarkable achievement that within a few years of freedom in Canada they were able to successfully organise churches, schools and societies. Blacks, once fed on a diet of warped Christianity, were able to transform their negative religious experiences in the United States into a dynamic, forceful ministry in Canada. Black leaders in Canada were able to successfully continue the efforts of the White clergy in providing a high quality of leadership at the organisational level.

Both education and religion were denied to most Blacks in the United States. An illustration is in 1841, when Francis Henderson, a former member of the Methodist Church in Washington D.C, was once warned by his master (a member of the Church of England), "you shan't go to that church -they'll put the devil in you."[6] Due to illiteracy, the beliefs and values of the enslaved community were passed on via the mediums of storytelling, preaching, songs and music. These served to reinforce societal values and Bible stories.[7]

Donald Wright, a researcher, noted that in the United States, "...slave owners refused to allow their bondsmen to worship by themselves for fear of the "mongrelization" of Christian practices they thought was bound to occur."[8] Some Southern Whites allowed their enslaved the freedom to worship without supervision.[9] Even those Blacks with limited religious freedom were excluded from the religious teachings of their masters. This was the case of Benedict Duncan who recalled, "My master and mistress belonged to the Presbyterian Church but never gave me any insight into their doctrines. I became a Methodist."[10] Thus, with some exposure to religion, the task of the White and later Black missionaries was to primarily eradicate religious misconceptions. The community proved to be the ideal environment in which educating and nurturing of the enslaved occurred.

The notion of inadequacy among fugitive Blacks was evident in one account in Amherstburg, "They were professed of many crude and wild notions...Hence from never having any religious discipline they are in a sad plight."[11] There were exceptions such as David West and Henry

Atkinson, who sought refuge at St. Catharines. Whilst in the United States they were allowed religious instruction on Sundays. Similarly, William Humbert, formerly of Charleston, South Carolina was also granted the opportunity to attend church on the Sabbath. Planters in states as South Carolina did not educate the enslaved as they felt it was associated with a rebellious spirit. A planned uprising of the enslaved in 1822 had supposedly originated at an AME Church in Charleston. Subsequently, authorities felt proper religious teaching would allow for a greater control of the Black population. Thus, the Methodist Church in South Carolina was allowed to spread Christianity among the Blacks.

Evidence that Blacks had formulated a crude concept of religion and possessed knowledge of a Supreme Being, is illustrated in the 1856 correspondence between two Blacks residing in Hamilton, to their family in the United States, "...tel them to remember my love to my church and brethren, tel them I find there is the same prayer-hearing God heare as there is in old Va."[12] It seemed that the optimism of the Blacks towards religion had not been radically transformed with their migration to Canada. Those Blacks with some form of religious freedom in the United States proved to be an asset to leadership in Canada.

Emergence of Black leaders

In Canada, free Blacks and former enslaved persons were eager to immerse themselves in Christianity. The sterling leadership qualities of Blacks proved to be an invaluable asset as separate churches were established. The demand for a local clergy was easily met as Blacks from the United States arrived in Canada and quickly became leaders in the various Protestant denominations:

> ...a quite natural path to leadership among Negroes was through the church; and those who wished to be preachers– whether for God or for themselves– saw quickly enough that they much improved their chances for success and tightened the circle of their followers if they narrowed the range of competition. Few churches at the time were prepared to see Negroes become bishops, deacons, or priests....[13]

This feature of gravitating towards leadership roles was especially true for Blacks professing the Baptist faith. One of the early Black religious pioneers was Elder Wilks who in 1818 embarked on a path of preaching, converting and baptising among Black communities. Wilks held the distinction of being the first ordained Black Baptist minister in

Canada and to have organised the first Black Baptist Church in Upper Canada.[14]

Missionary work was continued by Elder Washington Christian who founded Baptist churches among Blacks throughout Upper Canada, including those at St. Catharines, Hamilton and Toronto. As early as 22 March 1838, Christian adeptly mobilised Blacks to form a Baptist Church at St. Catharines. By 1847, Christian was heavily involved in preaching the Word of God through missionary tours of Chatham, Sandwich, Colchester and the Detroit region.[15] Also of this genre was Elder Anthony Binga, (referred to as Father Binga) another stalwart in the Baptist faith, who founded many of the Baptist churches in Canada West. One of the important contributions of Binga was his promotion of Christianity among the small, isolated Black settlements such as Mt. Pleasant, Puce and North Buxton.[16]

There is additional evidence of the leadership potential of Blacks. First, Benjamin Miller, originally from St. Louis, Missouri who served as pastor among the Methodists in London.[17] Second, Elisah Valentine had attained personal liberation through a hazardous trek which involved journeying from North Carolina to Ohio then to Canada. He utilised his potential to achieve the status as a deacon in the Baptist Church at Amherstburg.[18]

Itinerant Black preachers from the United States were experienced in the art of preaching and conducting worship services as their brethren in Canada. Their role was not merely to fill vacancies among the Black churches but signalled a dire need for hardworking preachers who would forge vibrant congregations. For instance, members of clergy serving at the First Baptist Church at Amherstburg included Revs. A. Binga (1836-1857, 1865), R.M. Huling (1866) and Fairfax (1870). In the early history of the First Baptist Church at Puce there was a regular supply of spiritual leaders- Father Binga and Elders Foot, Hodgekiss, Washington, Holliday and Anthony Binga Jr.[19] In Nova Scotia, areas with Black settlements as Tracadie, Digby, Preston, Halifax and Birchtown would be regularly visited by Black preachers.[20]

The travelling preacher was a common sight among Black communities. Two illustrations include Rev. R. Gordon, a coloured from London who belonged to the English Episcopal Church. He preached at Montreal on behalf of the fugitive Blacks. Secondly, Jeremiah Taylor dutifully served as circuit preacher of the AME Church.[21] Indeed, Canada's overall material progress during the nineteenth century contributed to an increased demand for personnel with redeeming leadership qualities and reflected a flurry of religious activity among Black churches. The contribution of foreign and local leaders exposed Blacks to a variety of lively preaching styles and fiery sermons.

The foreign and local contributions of missionaries strengthened and ensured Black leadership would have a positive impact on the settlements. Upon separation of the Black churches and the transfer of leadership from the Whites, some of the priorities among Blacks included the formation of organisations, sharing human resources and seeking solidarity. The subsequent exchange and movement of religious leaders among provinces, townships between Canada and the United States was not an uncommon feature by mid-nineteenth century. The Blacks from the United States sought to preserve their religious traditions.[22] This leadership interchange was particularly important as Black settlements were scattered in outlying rural areas as Galt, Gosfield, Hamilton and Windsor (see Appendix D). In the post-1840 era, the flowering of Baptist churches demanded more visitations of longer duration which attracted missionaries from abroad, thus highlighting the need for the development of local talent.[23]

The first female preacher of the First AME Church, Jareena Lee of New Jersey, visited Canada and preached at various venues. In 1843 she visited Niagara and preached to a group from the AME Connexion. However, six years later, the pastor for the church had died, the chapel no longer existed and the congregation had dispersed. Lee recounted preaching three times at Niagara and in 1849 visited St. David where she ministered to a congregation of both Blacks and Whites.[24] At Fort George she spoke on a Sunday morning, in a schoolhouse, to a congregation of Blacks and Whites. Lee expressed dismay to realise that at Chatham the believers were scattered and "without a shepherd."[25] At Amherstburg she recalled her response to a group of 25 children and young people, "I lamented their obscurity and advised them to get a white man to teach them, and endeavored to shew them, that, without the advantages of education they never would be a moral people...."[26] The reports from Chatham and Amherstburg suggest a failure in Black leadership and it was surprising that she suggested they seek a White leader.

By 1847, Rev. Samuel Davis (from Detroit) arrived as head of the Second Baptist Church and attended the Canadian sessions of the Baptist Association. Almost a decade later, in 1858, Davis was appointed pastor of the new Baptist Church in Chatham and continued to faithfully serve as moderator and clerk for fifteen and nineteen years respectively.[27] Similarly, James Holly, rector of St. Luke's Church in New Haven, Connecticut came to Canada during the period 1849-1850 to assist in the editing of the Black newspaper *Voice of the Fugitive*. The input of foreign Black talent seemed continuous, for example, Elder T.J. Henderson from the United States was stationed at Essex County and humbly served as pastor at various churches in Sandwich, Windsor, Gosfield, Chatham, Shrewsbury and Amherstburg. Others who assisted in the Lord's vineyard included Rev. William Newman, a Baptist minister from Virginia, who was appointed in 1845 by the American Baptist Free Mission Society to Upper Canada. Rev. Newman's brief stint at the Dawn Institute included leadership of the Baptist congregation in Toronto and Secretary of the Canadian Anti-Slavery Baptist Association.[28]

Sometimes the ministers serving Blacks were not considered proper role models. Included among this genre was Elder Isaac Rice, a Presbyterian missionary from New York, who was appointed by the AMA to serve as the spiritual leader of the Amherstburg Association.[29] Rice, who departed the United States in 1838, also conducted a Black school at Queen's Bush settlement, located north of the town of Guelph. However, Rice seemed different and Winks described him as "a strange, distant, and often pathetic figure" who was "unsympathetic" and "unbusinesslike."[30] Unfortunately, Rice was affected by cholera, poverty and personal problems, "...Rice was maddeningly tactless and inconsistent, for his disregard for religious labels was contrary to his own religious enthusiasms, and his willingness to accept help from any source contradicted his extremist views on slavery."[31]

Rice continued his work among Blacks but faced severe criticisms from the *Provincial Freeman,* "His notorious lying and begging have been frequently protested against by fugitives and colored people generally in this country...."[32] In 1855, Mary Ann Shadd condemned Rice's character and his "system of begging" in the United States for the Amherstburg mission. Shadd argued that his efforts:

> ...has a tendency to degrade the colored people and swindle their friends out of their money...and it is commonly reported that things which have been sent here for distribution...have been sold and the poor fugitives have got nothing, but a few old clothes.[33]

In 1850, Rev. David Hotchkiss, a Wesleyan Methodist minister, was appointed to replace Isaac Rice at the Amherstburg mission.

Another poignant illustration is Rev. Taylor in Toronto who was severely condemned for "disgusting, abusive and indecent language" and deplorable character:

> If our people choose, or even tolerate such men as their pastors...then we are the miserably low, degraded set that we said to be...the greatest dunces we have are our most acceptable preachers. Our conference impose on us,

by sending such elders as Taylor and a meeting such as he holds is a downright disgrace.[34]

Not surprisingly, Shadd favoured the British rather than United States missionaries whom she contemptuously described as being intolerant of Blacks:

> Many people here feel, they but change masters, the change is from physical shackles to those of moral and religious character....We love to think of what some good missionaries of the British societies are doing here...but deliver us and our people from Yankee missionaries, such as we have met in Canada, with smooth words, and hearts full of Negro-hate.[35]

This criticism from Shadd was a significant aspect in the development of Black leaders. Steven Hoogerwerf identified resistance as the medium in which Christian character was shaped. He believed that actual alternative sites of formation which challenge determinative cycles of cultural reproduction could be created by resistance.[36] This resistance displayed by the enslaved arose due to their realisation that they were not comfortable in the environment which influenced their daily lives.

In examining the nature of Black leadership, it is apparent that Blacks who emerged as leaders were influenced by the White ministers of the Protestant churches. Black leaders were initially inexperienced; but gradually improved their skills by patterning the White leaders and their church organisation. Winks believed this Black leadership was "not progressive" as it resulted in "...a single Negro whom whites treated as the sole local spokesman for the entire black community...and who might well be tempted not to lead along paths that would lose him white support."[37] It certainly seemed that the Whites sought to maintain a Black figurehead to ensure "the natural conservatism of the Negroes' churches."[38]

To a certain extent, the initial exchange between Black and White missionaries in United States and Canada contributed to the overall development of leadership amongst Blacks. Not surprisingly, a similar situation arose, in the United States among Black leaders as they were not only trained by White ministers but they were deprived of freedom of speech as their sermons often had to be approved by their masters or the White clergy. Likewise, the spirituals of the enslaved in the United States were modelled on those of the Whites but the wording of the songs had been modified to emphasise their desire for liberation.[39]

Blacks in the United States were gradually allowed religious independence. For instance, Whites of the First Baptist Church in Richmond relocated to a new building in 1841, and agreed that Blacks in their congregations could use the old building as a church. However, the Whites continued to hold the deed until 1866 and Blacks were initially unable to act as trustees of the First African Baptist Church. In the post-Civil War era, the White members of this First Baptist Church continued to financially assist their Black brethren.[40] Similarly, free Blacks at St. Paul's AME Church in Raleigh, began as a separate congregation in 1848 and were guided by a White minister from their parent church.[41] It seemed that even after slavery ended, Blacks in Canada continued to have more religious independence than Blacks in the United States.

In Canada, the transferring of the reins of religious power from White to Black religious leaders undertook a different path. The absence of slavery in Upper Canada in the post-1820s meant Black leaders were able to have much more freedom in their churches than their counterparts in the United States. It also meant that the gradual dissolution of ties with White parent churches needed to be handled diplomatically so as not to offend leaders and congregations.

This freedom allotted to Blacks served to strengthen their Protestant faith as they were given responsibility and had to prove their ability to be independent and worthy of their role as spiritual leaders. There was an interesting case of Black Baptists converting Whites. As early as 1836, there was a report of Whites residing near Siddall's Mills and Welsh, who belonged to the Baptist faith as a result of them being, "the converts of Paul the black man in Biddulph."[42] During 1840-1860 in South Carolina, there were instances of White Methodist preachers having to undergo training under Black ministers whose preaching abilities were well-known and respected.[43]

It should not be assumed that the separation of Black churches or schools meant Black leaders were unique or different from their White counterparts. Due to the paternalism of White churches, Canadian Blacks were strongly influenced in shaping the future of Black Protestantism. Apart from minor differences, the doctrines, interpretation of Scripture and institutional structure of both Black and White churches were similar. This reinforced the belief that the spirituality among Blacks was no different from that of Whites.

One outcome of the development of Black Protestantism in Canada was the role of Blacks as decision makers. Prominent Blacks involved at the forefront of church matters included Elder J. Hubbs, pastor at Sandwich Church in 1843, who was one of the first men to persuade the Baptist Association to break ties with its mother church in the United States. Additionally, in 1869 Elder J. H. Larter, pastor at Windsor Church, was privileged to spearhead the increase of the Association's outreach activities which resulted in the establishment of a vibrant Missionary Board.[44] Decisions among Blacks were milestones as it tested the mettle of the Black church in Canada. Thus, in addition to ministerial duties such as preaching and tending to the sick, the leaders were also expected to complement their preaching duties by making sacrifices of time and effort for church activities. Their presence on religious boards and committees allowed for a better utilisation of scarce leadership resources but unfortunately increased the workload of Black leaders.

In reconstructing the transition of religious power, an admirable feature of White leaders which Blacks imitated was their initiative in fund-raising efforts. During the 1840s, the clergy made a concerted effort in appealing for money for the upkeep of the all-Black settlements. Two prominent figures, Revs. Henson and Hiram Wilson, spearheaded the fund-raising initiatives of the Dawn Institute.[45] Henson made frequent trips across the border visiting such states as New York, Connecticut, Massachusetts, Boston and Maine seeking financial support.[46]

In a transatlantic visit to England, Henson established contacts at secular and religious levels and was granted an audience with Lord Grey and the Archbishop of Canterbury both of whom sympathised with the struggles of the settlement.[47] Apart from the overseas support, the local initiatives of the clergy's fund-raising schemes included such efforts as the Wesleyan Mission's weekly meetings in January 1850 at Sandwich, Colchester and Amherstburg.[48] This responsibility of obtaining resources proved vital in the continued survival of the Black mission stations.

Apart from the Baptists, the Methodists also made noteworthy contributions at the leadership levels in their churches. The presence of Black Methodism in Upper Canada can be traced to 1834 when ministers, from the United States, representing the AME Church arrived to preach to the Blacks.[49] Spiritual and physical growth of the churches not only demanded more Black leaders but demonstrated the necessity and maintenance of a high calibre of leadership to meet the increasing demands of congregations.

The delayed transferring of leadership from White to Black Protestant leaders was expected in the United States. Howard Rabinowitz in *Race Relations in the Urban South 1865-1890* noted that Black churches in the United States were founded by missionaries from the North who came South with Union troops, "Although the churches founded by the Northerners began with white pastors, by the end of the period blacks generally had taken their place."[50] In Canada, as early as 1834 at Amherstburg, Blacks were appreciative of vibrant leadership and this is best illustrated in Rev. Slight's account, "a leader amongst the people of colour called and expressed his high satisfaction at seeing and hearing a missionary."[51] Others as Rev. S. Ward, a coloured preacher from Toronto, lectured on slavery at a Methodist chapel in Elora.[52] Likewise, Rev. Solomon Hale, a Black from Hamilton, gave a lecture on slavery in the United States, to a receptive audience in Elora.[53] The Canadian Black population benefitted from religious revivals which accompanied the brief visits and boasted of similar enthusiastic responses among their churches.

After one of its revival services in 1853, the Coloured Wesleyan Methodist Church experienced a welcome increase of 100 communicant members.[54] Similarly, in 1867, the Amherstburg Baptist Church undertook a revival which attracted 80 converts.[55] Certain leaders ensured weekly services were publicised in the local press to inform the public, for example, the *Amherstburg Courier* advertised the Wesleyan Sabbath services at Colchester and Amherstburg.[56]

Not all Protestant missions among Blacks were success stories. For instance, despite the overwhelming contribution of the Anglicans to education at the provincial level, by 1854, they had failed to attract a considerable percentage of Blacks, which raised concerns among such leaders as Rev. Strachan:

> In regard to the coloured population we have made several attempts to draw them towards us but without effect- they seem suspicious of all interference & very ignorant and bigotte- moreover they seem all to belong to some denomination more or less opposed to the Church & few or none belong to us....[57]

The extent of Christianity among Black settlements partly depended on the response of Blacks in terms of converts and new mission stations. Undoubtedly, the expansion of churches hastened the development of Black leaders.

Through sermons Blacks were fed a constant diet of reminders about their safe deliverance unto the 'Promised Land' and the need to be ever grateful to their benefactors. One such sermon delivered by Henson at Fort Erie, emphasised the need to be ever mindful of family and friends still in bondage and their obligation to God.[58] A similar situation arose in the United States, as Black leaders with charisma, oratorical skills and insightful styles of preaching greatly contributed to the stability of settlements.[59] Indeed, charismatic pastors of Black churches in the United States shaped the lives of their congregations and thus "exercised a measure of internal social control."[60] Black leaders, like some Whites, provided an invaluable service in maintaining the racial harmony which prevailed among the Black settlements and certainly was a boon to the assimilation process.

Discipline, Morals and Ethics

In assessing the religious progress among Blacks, an indicator is the ability of their leaders to maintain and increase congregations. Thus, the exemplary character of elders, deacons and ministers was necessary if morale was to be boosted for winning converts for the expansion of the church ministry. The first generation of Black leaders belonged primarily to the Baptist and Methodist faiths and were able to admirably handle the reins of leadership. Vociferous on the pulpit and a master at social relations, these Black leaders served as remarkable role models and ensured the social fabric of Black and mixed communities were intact. However, Black leaders cannot accept all the credit for the exemplary moral qualities of the Black population. The actual experience of freedom from slavery had a positive effect which is evident from Howe's observation, "That with freedom and the ownership of property, the instinct of family will be developed, marriages will increase."[61] Thus, the role of Black leaders was not a solitary factor in the shaping of the Black's religious life but the earlier transition to freedom proved to be influential as well.

Authoritative advice emanating from Black leaders served to accentuate the spiritualism of Blacks and prevented an increase of backsliding members and absences on the Sabbath. In Canada, the Black congregations were generally well-disciplined and this is indicative of a people influenced by religion and appreciative of the joys of freedom. The religious nature of Blacks offered little reason for harsh reprimands and complimented the efforts of its leaders.

There was a correlation between quality leaders and the continued survival of the Black Protestant churches and settlements. Improperly trained and inexperienced White leaders would have ultimately produced poorly trained Blacks leading to the eventual collapse of the Black mission. An illustration is Henson who was at the centre of controversies:

> When he brought some polished boards to Boston to sell, as the first products of Dawn's sawmill, he accepted payment for them from Arnos Lawrence and his friends without crediting the sale against the original loan extended by the same group; and he failed to answer repeated requests from them for a promised note acknowledging his continued indebtedness.[62]

In August 1847 and 1848, at a Convention of Coloured Persons, held at Drummondville in Canada West, Henson was questioned on the state of financial affairs of the Dawn Settlement. However, an audit of the Institute's books proved that he could not be implicated for the mismanagement of funds.[63]

Soon after this episode, in June 1849, Henson was under scrutiny for his inadequate leadership at the settlement. Furthermore, in 1851 a group of Blacks in Chatham claimed that Henson was not their agent and thus had no authority to solicit money for Black Canadians and also that he did not establish a Black settlement in Canada. The Chatham Blacks accused Henson of being "totally unworthy" and "proved false" in dealing with funds.[64] It seemed like a plot to discredit Henson but he remained unperturbed. In 1849, whilst on a fund-raising trip in England, the British and Empire Anti-Slavery Society formed the London Investigative Committee and appointed John Scoble (Secretary of the Society) to investigate rumours surrounding Henson and the Dawn Settlement. On 12 July 1852, the Committee passed resolutions that Henson was the rightful agent of the Settlement and that the charges against him were false.

The Settlement's decline was temporarily halted in 1850 when the Board of the American Baptist Free Mission Society assumed control of its religious education. Subsequently, in 1852 the Baptists and the Foreign Anti-Slavery Society took control of the British American Institute and appointed John Scoble as manager. Mismanagement continued to plague the Institute and it eventually closed in 1868. Its lands were sold and the proceeds were used to erect the Wilberforce Educational Institute which was not segregationist. Most of the residents either moved to other communities in the province or returned to the United States.[65] Despite the accusations, Henson believed in peaceful resolutions rather than resorting to anti-social actions. In 1858, at an anti-slavery convention in Massachusetts, Henson opposed a motion which called for armed insurrection and immediate violent action to protest against slavery. Charles Remond, a Garrisonian activist, favoured a violent approach and criticised Henson as cowardly.

During the early 1840s, precautionary measures were adopted by the church and its Black leaders to prevent an abuse of power and privilege during this historic transition of power from the Whites. Church-related incidents deemed injurious to the well-being of the Black churches were temporal in nature. Thus these had an insignificant negative impact on the well-being of the churches.[66] Such situations were akin to the Protestant Blacks in the United States who were close-knit and tended to avoid the pitfalls of gossiping among members.[67]

In Upper Canada, the enforcement of harsh disciplinary measures by Black churches was rare and when such incidents arose, they were handled amicably and in good faith. In 1852 at the fourteenth Annual AME Conference, for the Canada District held at Bethel Church, St. Catharines, there was a query concerning the status of a member's attendance but this was quickly resolved:

> Brother Stevens brought a complaint against Brother Keith for neglecting to meet the annual conference of which he is a member. Brother Keith readily acknowledged his wrong, and promised faithfully to amend in the future; whereupon it was on motion resolved...and hereby is acquitted of the complaint.[68]

There was also a complaint against Paul O'Banyan for failing to attend the annual conference for five years but the case was postponed due to the absence of the accused.[69]

It should not be assumed that the overwhelming response of Blacks to Christianity meant an absence of disciplinary measures. A common method was the issuing of dismissal letters who threatened to usurp the status quo. For instance, in the 1843 minutes of the Amherstburg Baptist Association, 2 of its 5 churches used this procedure to discipline unruly members. Amherstburgh issued twelve dismissal letters whilst the church at Sandwich saw it fit for that two members face disciplinary charges.[70] There was a concerted effort to monitor the attendance and church involvement of members and this is exemplified in the constitution of the Canadian Anti-Slavery Baptist Association which outlined certain measures such as Article 4 "...to preclude from a seat in its meetings, minister or delegate who is manifestly corrupt either in theory or practice."[71] At the fourteenth Annual Conference of the BME Church, one of the first items on the agenda was discipline. Questions were raised regarding the preachers on trials, those who withdrew were expelled from the ministry.[72] The existence of church discipline reduced the incidence of a lackadaisical attitude amongst Black churches and demonstrated their ability and potential to effectively govern. Such peaceful resolving of issues had a positive influence on the settlements as stable Black family structures were buttressed.

It seemed that among Protestant churches the successful Black leadership rested partly upon the morals and ethics of Blacks. This was not always true among Black settlements in Canada. At Tracadie in Nova Scotia, the Roman Catholic Bishop, Joseph-Octave Plessis, identified 25 Black Protestant families who had been neglected by Protestant ministers and were eager for an English-speaking priest.[73] In 1814, another Catholic priest, reported that Blacks visited his chapel and attended Sunday morning services. This was not evident in nearby Guysborough County where many Roman Catholic Acadians were less interested than the Protestants in preaching among the Blacks.[74]

One of the reasons for the successful transition of power from Whites to Blacks can be traced to the moral values attained during slavery in the United States. An analysis of the 'spirituals' of the Blacks revealed that they strived to incorporate such esteemed values as confidence, morality, integrity, discipline and hard work.[75] The development of Black deacons, elders and bishops in Canada was not an overnight process but gradually developed from the philosophy that Black communities should be financially independent and self-reliant. Carrying the torch of success from White Protestant leaders, these Black religious pioneers possessed and promoted values of cooperation and industriousness which were highly prized among the settlements. It can be argued that because of a deep Protestant faith the transition to Black leadership was successfully accomplished.

Blacks were willing to accept leaders who were becoming accustomed to the reins of spiritual leadership. Generally for a leader to succeed he or she needed an obedient following, and this was also relevant for the Church's mission among the Blacks. The constant obedience and disciplinary measures once demanded from their masters in the United States, were no longer enforced in Canada and the Blacks now pledged allegiance to their various Protestant denominations. Leaders were blessed with Black or racially mixed congregations who were receptive and willing to make the word of God part of their lives. In dispensing religious knowledge, White Protestant leaders did not view the Black population as empty vessels to be filled with knowledge but as a people to be moulded in the likeness of Christ. In 1869, Rev. Willis Nazrey, General Superintendent of the BME Church, advised fellow Black leaders on the importance of conveying religious messages, "Ministers of the gospel are teachers, and hence we are called upon to teach as well as to preach. Therefore I hope that every minister will give strict attention to his duty in this respect, and teach the people their duties."[76] This obedience demanded from their flock increased the chances of assimilation of Blacks in Canada.

An illustration of the positive reception to religion is evident in the account of John Holmes, from Virginia, who resided in London, Canada West during the 1850s. Interestingly, Holmes observed a respectable attendance of Black people at every church.[77] Such favourable reports also emanated from Dresden where the Black population, comprising mostly of Baptists and Methodists, were judged as possessing morals. A cursory analysis of the Black churches in Chatham during the period 1787-1865 revealed that in the Baptist and BME denominations there was the enforcement of biblical doctrines which imbued "a firm religious and moral tone to the Chatham Negro."[78]

Black leaders neither possessed visions of grandeur nor sought fame and popularity. They displayed humility and were armed with charisma, counsel and vitality. Undoubtedly, the mission of Black leaders was to simply serve the Black population to the best of their ability. Indeed, it was a time of reckoning. Despite being burdened with limited resources, unfamiliarity in a new land and faced with challenges such as illiteracy, Black leaders admirably proved themselves to be worthy of overcoming any obstacles. The internalisation of the mores of White leaders ensured the baton of religious leadership would leave an indelible impression upon the minds of Blacks who strived to make Christianity a reality in their communities.

A cadre of zealous, upright and open-minded leaders promoted assimilation in society and simultaneously emphasised the value of education among their flock. Education empowered the Black leaders to comprehend the Bible and be effective teachers in the mission schools. The development of these leaders played a role in the processes of assimilation and segregation of Blacks as distinctive, autonomous religious bodies would be injurious to assimilation, whereas racially-mixed religious institutions would increase their chances of adjusting to a new host society. Occasionally there was a call echoing the need for proper leadership. This was evident in a report to the Colonial Church and School Society in 1866 which emphasised the desirability of Black missionaries if the race is to be improved.[79]

The transition from White to Black leadership reflected the nature and quality of the Black leaders. The demand for separate Black churches resulted in a genre of talented and hardworking Blacks who were willing to make sacrifices and ensure the survival of the fledgling mission stations. The religious and secular education initiated by Whites served as a springboard and foundation for future Black leaders. And, though there were occasional instances of discrimination in schools and churches, Black leaders were indebted to a majority of their White counterparts.

Notes

[1] Those who undertook the perilous journey northward to Canada were neither heathens nor pagans. Additionally, there is no evidence indicating that these Blacks were agnostics or atheists.

[2] Earnest Bell, "History of the Black Church in Detroit as a Study in American Public Address" (PhD diss., Wayne State University, 1987).

[3] Jensen 25.

[4] Winks, *Blacks in Canada*, 339.

[5] John Blassingame, *The Slave Community: Plantation Life in the Antebellum South* (New York: Oxford University Press, 1979), 132.

[6] Drew 159. Henderson a 19 year-old from Washington D.C. was a Black in London, Ontario.

[7] Karen Massey, "Ritual Improvisation: A Challenge to Christian Education from the Nineteenth Century African-American Slave Community" (PhD diss., Southern Baptist Theological Seminary, 1991).

[8] Donald Wright, *African Americans in the Colonial Era: From African Origins Through the American Revolution* (Illinois: Harlan Davidson, 1990), 96-97.

[9] Wright, *African Americans in the Colonial Era*, 97.

[10] Drew 110. Duncan was a slave in Maryland for 28 years and escaped to Toronto.

[11] Drew 46.

[12] Letter to William Still, 7 March 1856. William Still, *The Underground Railroad* (Philadelphia: Porter and Coates, 1872), 292. Also Drew 135.

[13] Winks, *Blacks in Canada*, 339.

[14] *A History of the Amherstburg Regular Missionary Baptist Association*, 2-3.

[15] "Biographies" McCurdy Papers, AO.

[16] Binga was pastor of the Amherstburg Baptist Association 1841-1854. See also summary of Binga's life. "Reverend Anthony Binga Jr.," *Akili* 2 (1994): 14.

[17] Drew 188.

[18] See Rev. William Troy, *Hair Breath Escapes from Slavery to Freedom* (Manchester: np, 1861).

[19] 150th Anniversary brochure of the Baptist Church, Amherstburg. 1836-1986, 3. Also 113th Anniversary brochure of the First Baptist Church, Puce, 1864-1977, 1. CBA. For more on the genealogy of the Bingas see Jerome Teelucksingh, "The Bingas: A Coloured Family History," *Families* 42 (2003): 237-240.

[20] Elgersman 147.

[21] *London Free Press*, October 24, 1859. *Canadian Freeman*, November 21, 1846.

[22] Elgersman 147.

[23] "Biographies" McCurdy Papers, AO.

[24] "Religious Experiences and Journal of Mrs. Jareena Lee giving an Account of her call to preach the Gospel," in Henry Louis Gates Jr. ed. *Spiritual Narratives* (New York: Oxford University Press, 1988), 66.

[25] "Religious Experiences of Lee" 69.

[26] "Religious Experiences of Lee" 69.

[27] "Biographies" McCurdy Papers, AO.

[28] James Washington, "The Origins and Emergence of Black Baptist separatism 1863-1897" (PhD diss., Yale University, 1979), 53, 72-74, 80. See also Winks, *Blacks in Canada*, 196-198.

[29] Minutes of the 16th Anniversary of the Amherstburg Baptist Association held with the First Baptist Church at Chatham, Canada West, 11-14 September 1856 (Detroit, 1856), 3.

[30] Winks, *Blacks in Canada*, 197.

[31] Winks, *Blacks in Canada*, 198.

[32] *Provincial Freeman*, September 2, 1854.

[33] *Provincial Freeman*, June 30, 1855.

[34] *Voice of the Fugitive*, December 17, 1851.

[35] *Provincial Freeman*, June 24, 1854.

[36] See Steven Hoogerwerf, "Forming the Character of Christian Discipleship: Singing the Lord's Song in a Strange Land" (PhD diss., Duke University, 1991).

[37] Winks, *Blacks in Canada*, 340.

[38] Winks, *Blacks in Canada*, 340.

[39] Blassingame 132, 137.

[40] Howard Rabinowitz, *Race Relations in the Urban South 1865-1890* (New York: Oxford University Press, 1978), 199-200.

[41] Rabinowitz 200.

[42] Proudfoot Diary, 9 February 1836. Fred Landon Papers, University of Western Ontario.

[43] Stephen W. Angel, "Black Methodist preachers in the South Carolina Upcountry, 1840-1866- Isaac Cook, James Porter and Henry McNeal Turner," in Alonzo Johnson and Paul Jersild eds."*Ain't gonna lay my 'ligion down'-African American religion in the South* (Columbia: University of South Carolina Press, 1996), 93.

[44] "Biographies" McCurdy Papers, AO.

[45] *Christian Freeman* November 27, 1845.

[46] Henson, *Autobiography*, 126.

[47] Henson, *Autobiography*,142.

[48] *Amherstburg Courier*, January 5, 1850. There were acknowledgments in the newspapers of non-Black churches receiving financial contributions from the Governor General and other respected individuals. *Chatham Gleaner*, September 28, 1844.

[49] Methodism by 1860 seemed strong in North America:

Canadian Wesleyan Conference	43,672
Methodist Episcopal Church	13,352
AME Church	20,000
AMEZ Church	9,203

[50] Rabinowitz 202.

[51] Journal of Benjamin Slight, 11 August 1834. vol.1, 45. UCA.

[52] *Elora Backwoodsman*, July 1, 1852.

[53] *Lightning Express*, May 24, 1872.

[54] "Coloured Wesleyan Methodist Church History," 2. "Miscellaneous Notes" Abbott Papers, Metropolitan Library, Toronto.

[55] "Notes" McCurdy Papers, AO.

[56] *Amherstburg Courier*, January 5, 1850.

[57] Letter from Strachan to Rev. E. Dewar, November 2, 1854, 36. John Strachan Letter Book. Strachan Papers, AO.

[58] Josiah Henson, *Father Henson's Story of His Own Life With an Introduction by Mrs. H. Stowe* (Boston: John P. Jewett and Company,1858), 45. There is the belief that during the nineteenth century, Christianity gave the impression that "God was a God of order..." and that religion and culture gave to society stability and coherence. William Westfall, *Two Worlds: The Protestant Culture of Nineteenth Century Ontario* (Montreal: McGill-Queen's University Press, 1989), 15, 33.

[59] See Blassingame 131.

[60] Rabinowitz 199.

[61] Howe 103.

[62] Winks, *Blacks in Canada*, 196. Henson had promised one Protestant denomination that he would not accept assistance from members of another denomination and then promptly did so. And, in London, he spoke in support of emigration to the West Indies but denied this when he returned to Canada.

[63] Pease and Pease 64.

[64] Pease and Pease 65.

[65] Kelly 3.

[66] This is in contrast to the disciplinary measures of the White-dominated First Baptist Church at Brantford. See minutes of the Brantford Church which revealed the case of a member being expelled from the church membership because of intemperance, slander and falsehood. Minutes of the Church Meeting, June 5, 1860. Minute Book of the Proceedings of the Regular Baptist Church, Brantford, Canada West. In Brantford First Baptist Church Papers 1833-1876. vol 2. For other incidents of exclusion see Minutes of the Church Meeting June 26, 1853. Baldwin Room, Metropolitan Library, Toronto.

[67] Charles C. Jones, *The Religious Instruction of the Negroes in the United States* (Savannah, 1842), 125-127.

[68] Minutes of the AME Conference July 13, 1852, 2. McCurdy Papers, AO. *Voice of the Fugitive*, August 12, 1852.

[69] *Voice of the Fugitive*, August 12, 1852.

[70] Minute Book of the Amherstburg Baptist Association October 8, 1841, September 14, 1877. CBA.

[71] Canadian Anti-Slavery Baptist Association Constitution Article 4. See also Section 8 which omits any church from its Minutes that misses three consecutive meetings. CBA.

[72] *Voice of the Fugitive*, August 12, 1852.

[73] Elgersman 147.

[74] G.A. Rawlyk, "The Guysborough Negroes: A Study in Isolation," *Dalhousie Review* 1 (1968): 27.

[75] Jeremiah A. Wright, "The Treatment of Biblical Passages in Negro Spirituals" (MA thesis, Howard University, 1969), 133-169.

[76] Proceedings of the Thirteenth Session of the Annual Conference of the British Methodist Episcopal Church of the Dominion of Canada. 1869, 5. UCA.

[77] Drew 161.

[78] John Farrell, "The History of the Negro Community in Chatham, Ontario 1787-1865" (PhD diss., University of Ottawa, 1955), 189.

[79] "Mission to the Free Coloured Population" 1866, 5. By 1840, other denominations in Upper Canada were gradually demanding locally educated clergy. Grant 84.

CHAPTER FIVE

MIRACLES OF MANAGEMENT AND BLACK THEOLOGY

If a slave has taken refuge with you, do not hand him over to his master. Let him live among you wherever he likes and in whatever town he chooses. Do not oppress him (Deuteronomy 23:15-16)

In Canada, Black leaders were instrumental in spearheading the organisation of their churches. In 1802 at St. Catharines in Upper Canada, many of the Blacks migrated northward to Queenston, Fort Erie and Niagara-on-the-Lake. Following most of these formerly enslaved, "...came the circuit riders or minister of the Methodist Episcopal Church who organized bands or societies of believers in the various homes, or held meetings in some halls for Weekly Sunday services."[1] In the post-1812 period, fugitive Blacks who crossed the Detroit River were guided by the Thames River to Chatham and then to Lake Erie and Shrewsbury where they founded the First Baptist Church at Shrewsbury.[2]

In 1826 in Toronto, a group of refugee Blacks clamoured for a proper house of worship which eventually led to the establishment of the First Baptist Church by Elder Washington Christian. Likewise, in 1833 runaways, comprising enslaved persons from the United States, formed a congregation in Toronto which was located in Richmond Street, east of York Street. In 1851 this building was renamed Grant AME Church (in memory of Abraham Grant who later attained the position of bishop). Similar developments occurred in Amherstburg and Puce as increasing demands by Black refugees led to the founding of the Amherstburg Baptist Church and the First Baptist Church at Puce.[3]

At Hamilton in 1830, Henson encouraged formerly enslaved persons to build a church on Rebecca Street between Catherine Street and John Street. Subsequently, Bishop Willis Nazrey encouraged the new congregation to be affiliated to the AME Conference and the church was eventually renamed St. Paul's AME Church.[4] During the 1850s, the increasing number of fugitives forced the church to move to a new site. One of the better known churches in Chatham- the First Baptist Church, founded in 1841, which accommodated the meetings of fugitive Blacks from the United States.

The sacrifices of the members in the early history of these Black churches reflected their determination to succeed. At the First Baptist Church in North Buxton, the building was not easily accessible due to inadequate roads and church meetings were conveniently continued at homes and in a nearby school.[5] Likewise, worship services of the Zion Baptist Church at St. Catharines (founded 1838) were initially held in homes and schools.[6] Among the Black Baptists, their edifices for worship were simple and whilst some comprised log structures as in Colchester and Puce others were small, inconspicuous buildings as in Chatham.[7] In Hamilton, the St. Paul's AME Church (now Stewart Memorial Church) was originally housed in a log structure. During this period, there were instances of shared accommodation among the denominations. At Puce, the First Baptist Church erected in 1846 shared the building with the Methodists. And, as the Baptist membership increased, there was a growing demand for regular worship services which led to a separate church.[8]

Often the attainment of organisational independence for Black churches was not a smooth transition, as illustrated with the Middlesex and Elgin Association of Baptist Churches. In 1829, the Western Association was formed with 10 churches and the first annual meeting carded for 1830. This Association included the African Church of Wilberforce and the First African Church of Colchester. However, all was not well and in 1837 a schism soon developed with the separation and formation of the Long Point Association which included the African Baptist Church of St. Thomas.

In 1841, the formation of the Amherstburg Association was not favourably received by the Long Point Baptist Association. Two years later, the latter refused to recognise the fellowship of the Amherstburg Association. The Long Point Baptist Association was a conference of White Baptist churches which were involved in controversies regarding the refusal of its member church, at St. Thomas, to accept Blacks into its fold. On 8 October 1841, the Sandwich Church and Second Baptist Church of Detroit convened a meeting and subsequently agreed that their organisation should be referred to as the "Amherstburg Baptist Association for Colored People" (Rev. Binga is credited as having founded the Amherstburg Baptist Association).[9] In October 1841, delegates from Detroit, Sandwich and Amherstburg met at the home of John Liberty, at Amherstburg, and agreed that they were unable to "enjoy the Privileges we Wish as Christians with the White Churches in Canada."

Subsequently, an international association was formed with member churches from Niagara and South London to Detroit.[10]

During the second annual session of this Association, held at the First Baptist Church of Amherstburg, representatives agreed to adopt the new name- "Amherstburg Baptist Association."[11] From its inception there was a conscious attempt to create and maintain a respectable cadre of religious leaders as ministers and elders who were forbidden to preach if they were morally unfit and alcoholics.[12] In the colourful history of the Amherstburg Baptist Association, like other Black churches, it experienced fluctuations in membership and was faced with internal dissension.[13]

By 1845, both the Western and Long Point Baptist Associations were re-united under the banner of the Western Association. However, this union was only temporary and fourteen years later there was a major division as 29 churches departed from the Western Association to form the Middlesex and Elgin Association.[14] During that year disputes arose between the Long Point and the Amherstburg Baptist Associations. Despite this factionalism, the growth of both groups was not affected; and in 1847 the Amherstburg Association benefitted from the addition of two new churches- the First Regular Baptist Church of Colchester and the First Baptist Church of Hamilton.[15] Three years later, the Amherstburg Baptist Association encountered certain challenges as the Colchester Church reported a decrease in membership and the Chatham Church was rejected from the Association. Additionally, the Second Baptist Church of Detroit eventually ended ties with the Association and joined the Canadian Antislavery Baptist Association whilst the Mount Pleasant Baptist Church was refused membership.[16] Robin Winks strongly disagreed with the notion that the Black Baptist churches possessed any semblance of coherence:

> ...the Negro churches remained divisive, schismatic, petty feudatories based upon isolated and impoverished followings....A tendency toward litigiousness, insistence on a narrow doctrinal "soundness," and divided and unstable leadership slowed Negro progress, seemed to confirm white prejudices, and undermined any possibility of black power within the wider Baptist church, itself divided by evangelical and credal controversies.[17]

Upon retrospection, it seemed that Winks should have considered the lack of previous experience and proper training of these Blacks who sought to create and maintain separate churches.

The apparent instability of the Black churches seemed a temporary phenomenon. The 1850s ushered in a reversal of fortunes for the Amherstburg Association. Minor differences with the Chatham Church were amicably settled, and in 1853 the Amherstburg Association and Long Point Association (known as Western Association) also resolved their problems.[18] From 1854-1856, three churches sought admission into the Association- the New Canaan Baptist Church, Little River Baptist Church and Windsor Church. Shortly afterwards, a disagreement arose between the Amherstburg Association and the Canadian Anti-Slavery Baptist Association. Nevertheless, in 1857, the uniting of the Amherstburg Association and the Canadian Antislavery Baptist Association strengthened the presence of the Baptists in Upper Canada. This favorable trend continued with the welcoming of other churches into the fold–the Second Baptist Church of London, Shrewsbury and Dresden Churches.[19] There was a brief increase in membership as the Amherstburg Association had 13 churches and 763 members in 1860; one year later, the total membership had increased to 14 churches with 1060 members.[20] During 1862-1863, Gosfield Church (formerly belonging to the Western Association) and Puce Church were admitted into the Amherstburg Association.[21]

In 1832, Richard Preston returned to Halifax, Nova Scotia and assumed control of the Black Baptist Church. Subsequently, he spearheaded the formation of the Black Abolition Society in 1846. On 14 April 1832, in Nova Scotia, the first Baptist Church established branches at Hammonds Plains, Dartmouth, Preston and Beach Hill.[22] The name of the church was later changed to Cornwallis Street Baptist Church. In 1853 at Granville Mountain, Preston initiated a conference which resulted in the founding of the African United Baptist Association (AUBA). This subsequently became a central institution in the lives of Black Nova Scotians. As a consequence of these developments, "The church would be the source of spiritual succour and the focus of educational, cultural, social and political activities throughout all the Black communities."[23] During 1854-1860, Septimus Clarke served as the first clerk of the AUBA. Preston founded churches at Salmon River, Bear River, Digby, Hammonds Plains and Weymouth.

The relative absence of a haphazard and chaotic atmosphere among the Black churches in upper Canada was partly due to the rules governing the various religious groups. For instance, the constitution of the Regular Baptist Association contained 10 Articles and 7 Rules of Order. These church documents outlined the general codes of conduct, frequency of meetings and requirements for admission into the Association. One illustration is Article 8 which stated that the Association would not interfere with the independence of the individual churches and Article 9 drew reference to the annual hosting of the Association and the session that was held for four days.[24]

There is a lack of evidence to determine the benefits and motivating factors of the members which persuaded them to allocate time to organise and attend these regional meetings. A simple faith in God seemed to have been a cornerstone in their involvement in the churches.[25] For example, the wording of the covenant of the First Baptist Church at Sandwich stressed the importance of being morally upright, "...to walk in our house as becometh those profeing godlinef to maintain the worship of God in our families, and to train those under our care in the way of religion and virtue."[26] There were certain acts in this covenant which served as religious guidelines such as Act 11 which advised members "...to watch over each other according to the rules of the Gospel," and Act 18 which prescribed, "we believe that it is the duty of Church members to bear their equal proportion." The criteria for spiritual membership in the church was strongly related to the Biblical teachings as Act 16 professed, "we believe that in all ordinary cases of transgrefion, the rule given by Jesus Christ in the 18th Chapter of Matthew should be observed." The adherence to such guidelines served to forge closer bonds among members as it made the church a congenial domain in which theology would become a reality in the lives of its members.

In Canada, the location and successful organisation of the Black churches was largely determined by the density of the Black communities. The major underlying reason for the formation of churches rested upon the demand for religious services from Blacks. Undoubtedly, the organisational ability of the Black church allowed it to survive the transition from White to Black leadership and make a monumental contribution.

The Canadian Blacks were aware of the advantages of hosting conferences and the importance of recording minutes. An insight into the records of church organisation clearly indicated that Blacks independently and successfully managed their internal affairs. The African Methodist Episcopal Zion (AMEZ) Church began its work in Canada in 1829 and almost three decades later, in 1860, the AMEZ General Conference had five representatives from Canada. After this church's expansion into Michigan, the conference was referred to as the Canada-Michigan Conference (the title 'Michigan Conference' was later adopted). At the Michigan Conference, Bishop Blackwell founded churches in Wisconsin and was faithfully assisted by Revs. S.W. Walter and A.M. Taylor in Colchester, Upper Canada.[27]

The BME Church in Canada had an initial connection with the United States. In 1838, Bishop Brown of the AME Church arrived in Canada to organise the first annual conference and this paved the way for the fourteenth annual conference of the AME Church held at Bethel Church in St. Catharines.[28] At this historic conference, the delegates included the presiding Bishop- Rev. Willis Nazrey and two representatives from the United States.[29] By 1852 the membership and location of the various preaching stations of the BME Church highlighted the demand for capable and permanent Black leaders in Canada West to maintain scattered congregations (see Appendix E). This relationship materialised into a Canadian Conference of the AME Church which was under the watchful eyes of the parent body in the United States. Appeals for independence and self-governance resulted in the Canadian Conference of the AME Church.

The Black churches displayed initiative and on 29 September 1856, an independent church was established in Chatham known as the British Methodist Episcopal Church with Rev. Willis Nazrey being appointed as the first General Superintendent. Nazrey was not only credited as having founded the BME Church as well as churches throughout Canada and the West Indies.[30]

A similar development took place in the AME Church in Toronto in 1865 after 25 years in operation. The church sought permission for independence from the main branch at Philadelphia. And, on agreement, the church's name was changed from "African Methodist Episcopal" to "British Methodist Episcopal."[31] In the nineteenth century the growth of churches among the Black Methodists was a common feature among the White Methodists and the increase in membership and spread of churches made them one of the most successful denominations in Upper Canada.[32]

The supervision of the churches was critical. An overview of the annual conferences and sessions of the BME Church in Upper Canada suggested there was a regularity and consistency of meetings among the Black churches (see Appendices F and G). A similar phase of growth was evident in Nova Scotia and New Brunswick. In 1840, the seven Black Baptist churches had 273 members.[33] The regular assembly of Black churches witnessed the converging of representatives and one of the cohesive forces which ensured the survival of Black churches.

Undoubtedly, the decision to regularly host these meetings at different venues gave each region a sense of importance in the association. The annual gatherings, held at Windsor, Hamilton, London, St. Catherines, Toronto, Chatham and Brantford, established a precedent for other churches as the Coloured Wesleyan Methodist Church which held its conference at Dawn in 1851.

Despite the existence of associations and schools there were criticisms of the work of these churches. The *Provincial Freeman* condemned the apparent shortcomings of the Protestant denominations:

> ...teachers should have been selected from the religious denominations, TO WHICH THE PEOPLE BELONGED, among which they were to labour. It is a fact, that the colored people, of Canada, are almost entirely of the Baptist or Methodist persuasion, and nearly all the teachers sent among them have been either Presbyterians or Congregationalists. No one need wonder at their failure...But we must admonish our Baptist and Methodist friends...since they neglected their duty, and done but little or nothing for us....It is the error of the *missionaries generally* TO EDUCATE THE HEATHEN FIRST, in order to their becoming *Christians*, when they should make their Christians first, in order to their being *properly* educated.[34]

This observation was not an exaggeration but most likely a result of the overwhelming workload of the Methodists and Baptists. Undoubtedly, the Black Baptists and Methodists, with their limited resources, were overburdened with the responsibility of establishing churches whilst overseeing the moral and social welfare of the refugees. Both denominations were able to establish a strong presence in areas as Buxton and Raleigh Township (see Table 5-1). The legacy of the Black BME Church was not unique because the Amherstburg Baptist Association also displayed a similar discipline in their structure.

Table 5-1: Religious affiliation of Blacks in Buxton and Raleigh Township

	Buxton	Raleigh Township
Blacks Only	Number	Number
Methodist	381	309
Baptist	166	122
Presbyterian	127	57
Catholic	5	10
Anglican	1	3
Congregational	1	--
Quaker	10	10
No religion	8	44
Unknown	53	27
Total	752	582

Source: *Census of Canada, Raleigh Township*, 1861.

Financial and Attendance Records

The membership of the churches fluctuated for a number of reasons including the size of the Black community. The strength of the particular denomination and the search for jobs determined the success of the churches and settlements:

> The great mass of the colored people of Canada have been thrown entirely upon their own resources...there is positive and tangible proof of the will and the ability of the colored people to work and support themselves, and gather substance even in the hard climate of Canada.[35]

Sometimes due to the absence of historical sources, it is difficult to pinpoint the reason for the closure of a church. For instance, the First Baptist Church, at Talbot Street in Elgin County, operated for three decades before it suddenly closed in 1860.[36] Likewise, at Mt. Hope, the Baptist church abruptly ended in 1852 as a result of Blacks being attracted to government land grants. Attendance at annual meetings of the Amherstburg Association seemed to have generated considerable interest among the members of the church. A cursory examination of Table 5-2 reflects the fluctuation of the Association's membership.

Table 5-2: Membership of the various churches that joined the Amherstburg Association

	1843	1845	1847	1848	1849
Amherstburg	47	51	69	86	97
2nd Detroit	28	89	89	89	105
Sandwich	28	12	13	No Info	18
Chatham	9	10	21	25	27
Mt. Pleasant	10	10	16	16	11
Hamilton	No info	No info	36	35	32
Colchester	No info	No info	No info	No info	13

(Compiled from the minutes of the annual meetings of the Amherstburg Association 1843, 1845, 1847, 1848 and 1849 as recorded in the *Minute Book of the Amherstburg Association October 8, 1841-September 14, 1877*. pp.17, 34-35, 52-53, 65-66).

One of the hallmarks of the Black Baptist churches was their concerted efforts to record financial transactions. The minute books from 1846-1874 of the First Baptist Church at Windsor revealed documented details of purchases towards the upkeep of property. The records of 1852

Table 5-4: Religious affiliation of Blacks in Chatham, 1851, 1861 and 1871

Denomination	1851	1861	1871	
Methodist	193	744	635	
Baptist	128	356	242	
Catholic	11	47	30	
Congregational	12	6	2	
Presbyterian	2	8	13	(includes Ch. of Scotland)
Anglican	-	67	15	
Free Thinker	-	2	1	
Disciples	-	15	-	
Shaker	-	1		
No religion	4	9		
Unknown	3	4		

(Source: *Census of Canada, Town of Chatham*, 1851, 1861, 1871)

The ability of the Black churches to procure donations and financial support from the public hinged on the projection of a trustworthy and stable image. Thus satisfactory organisation and performance were deemed essential for survival. Proof that the BME had attained a certain standard was evident in Charles Avery's will (of the County of Alleghany (sic) and State of Pennsylvania) which stated that funds had been promised to the BME Conference for educational purposes.[48] Undoubtedly, this act of generosity suggested that the work of the BME Church in Upper Canada was favourably received.

Black Theology

Without the independence and organisation of the Black churches in Canada there would have been either a skewed theological insight among Blacks or an absence of Black Theology. The rudimentary foundation of a Black Theology in Canada had been initiated by the enslaved from the United States. The enslaved persons erected "invisible houses" or congregated in special cabins dubbed "praise houses" to hold clandestine meetings and to worship. Cheryl Sanders noted that the religion of the enslaved was a response to the evils of slavery. She argued that on the basis of Christian ethics, Blacks rejected slavery.[49] There was a moral dilemma as the enslaved had to decide if there should be passive acceptance of the oppressive system or active resistance to end slavery. In the United States, during the post-slavery era, the segregation of the

Blacks in churches inevitably contributed to a unique spiritual development.

A similar argument can be made for the Black presence in Canada. Indeed, the concept of a Black Theology gradually emerged when Black congregations openly rejected racist Biblical interpretations and attitudes of the White churches. Black Theology was rooted in the Black community and is considered a liberation theology through which socio-political strategies could be planned.[50]

During 1780-1830 Blacks in the United States were not excluded or marginalised from the 'Second Awakening' which swept across America. Due to the fact that White churches had exposed Blacks to the Christian world and ordained their clergy, the Black Baptist and Methodist missions developed strong parallels to the parent churches. The rise of the Black AME, Baptist, Methodist and AMEZ churches in North America was a response to the racist doctrines meted out by their White peers.[51] By 1860 the African population in the United States was 4,444,830 and from this total, 12% to 15% were enrolled as members of the Baptist and Methodist churches. During the Civil War there was a certain apocalyptic imagery in songs of the enslaved and the clergy's theological writings in the North and South. The upheavals in the 1860s led many of the enslaved to view themselves as the "second children of Israel" who would soon occupy a Promised Land.[52]

Some Whites were critical of the church services of Blacks which seemed too emotional and lacked intellectual content.[53] Winks contended, "The Negro's churches often lacked intellectual conviction while possessing an abundance of emotion and faith."[54] This is true as a result of adult Blacks not being exposed to religious learning and basic education whilst in the United States. However, the theological and intellectual shortcomings did not hamper the ambitions of Blacks as Winks admitted:

> ...the first organized Negro institution in a Canadian community usually was a church, followed by a temperance society and a school. These three institutions were to be found wherever there were Negroes, and they emphasized the pious, the puritan and the practical.[55]

The Black churches in Canada have been described by Winks as "fragments of Protestantism" which were "theologically stagnant."[56] Preston Washington contended that the composition of the Black Faith explains the simultaneous emergence of the Black religious imagination and the Black preacher in the United States. He described the Black faith as a hybrid entity with Judeo-Christian concepts mixed with traditional African cultic beliefs. Peter Paris in "The Spirituality of African Peoples" believed traditional African religions "absorbed Christianity into themselves thus transforming both."[57] In an interesting twist, Bobby Neeley argued that Voodooism was the basis for all Black religions in the United States. He identified aspects of music, songs, medicine and magic which indicated acculturation and retention of Voodooism.[58] Such views reinforced the belief that the enslaved maintained close ties with their African heritage.

Indeed, the unique feature of Black Christianity was partly due to the West African origins of Black spirituality in the United States.[59] This explained the religious creativity of the enslaved particularly among early Black preachers who blended ideas of psychic well-being with external social changes and internal identity formation.[60] At Locust Grove in Kentucky, the enslaved used religion and magic to strengthen community bonds and ward off bad-luck.[61] It was obvious that despite being Christians, the superstitious nature of enslaved persons had not disappeared.

One of the modes of worship which appealed to Black congregations was the music at religious services. This was observed by Rev. King, "The coloured people as a race are fond of music and some of them became celebrated as musicians."[62] In Upper Canada, this musical talent at religious services was not an overnight success but could be traced to the United States.

Music formed an integral part of worship in the Black churches in the United States. Many of these Black spirituals possessed liberation themes and reflected the consciousness of an oppressed people.[63] These religious songs partly contributed to providing an opportunity for individual interpretation and expression among the enslaved and free Blacks. In the United States, it was evident that religion among the Blacks was unique, "...the experiences of gathering, greeting, singing, testifying, dance, trance and collapse gave the people the re-intensified strength they need to face again the structured and often oppressive workaday world."[64] Increased religious feeling among Blacks was associated with spiritual death and rebirth.[65]

Some Blacks who arrived in Canada continued to incorporate this unique form of religious expression in their churches. This aspect of their religion added to the distinctiveness of worship in Black churches vis-à-vis worship in White churches.[66] Interestingly, one of the reasons that Blacks were attracted to the Methodist and Baptist faiths was the religious expression, "These denominations appealing to the soul and emotion had been very popular on the slave plantations, for their services provided a natural outlet for feelings of frustration."[67] Evidence of a particular denomination attracting Blacks partly due to their music was at Windsor. The majority of the Black congregations belonged to the Mount Zion churches and comprised descendants of former enslaved persons who escaped to Canada.[68] Such activities as drumming underwent a fusion of African and Christian musical forms. In North America, the Caribbean and Africa, the importance of music in the Black religions cannot be underscored. The emergence of this unique music reflected the bond between Christianity and Blacks.

In analysing the spirituality of the Buxton settlement, the religious life among Blacks in the Buxton settlement has been described as "vibrant and extensive" and "regardless of their denominational affiliation, Buxton residents were active spiritually, maintaining their churches and ministering to the local community."[69] Among Blacks, prevailing positive attitudes served as a fertile ground for sowing seeds of a rich spiritual life. In the post-slavery era in the United States, free Blacks and formerly enslaved were able to successfully and rapidly expand a network of churches with vibrant congregations.[70] They were able to boast of these accomplishments with no formal training and the minimum of resources.

Notes

[1] Origin of the BME Church of Canada in St. Catharines, Landon Papers, University of Western Ontario.
[2] A History of the Regular Baptist Missionary Association 4, 95. Letter from Rev. Thomas Berry to sister churches (dated 1964), CBA.
[3] A History of the Regular Baptist Missionary Association 4, 95. Letter from Rev. Thomas to sister churches, 1964. CBA.
[4] Jerome Teelucksingh, "Family Links with Baptists in the Amherstburg Association during the 1840s," *Families* 43 (2004): 37.
[5] History of the First Baptist Church, North Buxon, mimeo. CBA.
[6] A History of the Amherstburg Regular Missionary Baptist Association CBA.
[7] A History of the Amherstburg Regular Missionary Baptist Association 48. See also The History of the First Baptist Church, Chatham, November 1962, 1. CBA
[8] Teelucksingh, "Family Links with Baptists," 37.
[9] 125th Anniversary brochure of the First Baptist Church, Windsor; 84th Anniversary of the First Baptist Church, Windsor.
[10] Winks, *Blacks in Canada*, 342.
[11] 150th Anniversary brochure of the First Baptist Church, Amherstburg 1836-1986.
[12] Minute Book of Amherstburg Association, 8 October 1841-14 September 1877, 3, 5. In the Buxton mission there was reportedly not a drunkard among the settlers. *Provincial Freeman* March 24, 1854.
[13] In 1866 this group changed its title to the Amherstburg Regular Missionary Baptist Association.
[14] Elgin Association of Churches 1860-1969, Elgin Association of Baptist Churches-A History October 1967, 1-3. CBA. Shreve 66.

[15] *Pathfinders of Liberty and Truth*, 10.

[16] *Pathfinders of Liberty and Truth*, 14-15

[17] Winks, *Blacks in Canada*, 344.

[18] Shreve 68.

[19] *Pathfinders of Liberty and Truth*, 18.

[20] In 1861 leaders in the Amherstburg Association were William C. Monro, Madison Lightfoot and Anthony Binga.

[21] *Pathfinders of Liberty and Truth*, 19.

[22] Paris 12-13.

[23] "Black Nova Scotian odyssey," 84.

[24] Minutes of the 16th Anniversary of the Amherstburg Baptist Association held with the First Baptist Church at Chatham, Canada West, September 11-14, 1856 (Detroit, 1856). The Constitution of the Baptist Association contained 11 Articles and 8 Rules of Order. Minute Book of the Amherstburg Association October 8, 1841-September 14, 1877, 9-12. CBA.

[25] In West Africa and Egypt a God-consciousness was seen as a stabilising factor among settlements. James J. Gardiner and J. Deotis Roberts eds. *Quest for a Black Theology* (Philadelphia: United Church Press, 1971), 51.

[26] Covenant of the First Baptist Church, Sandwich 1846. CBA.

[27] William Walls, *The African Methodist Episcopal Zion Church-Reality of the Black Church* (North Carolina: AMEZ Publishing House, 1974), 131, 204, 223.

[28] Origins of the British Methodist Episcopal Church of Canada, taken from the Discipline of the British Methodist Episcopal Church, 1890, 1.

[29] Minutes of the AME Conference for the Canada District, July 10, 1852, 1. There two representatives from the United States were Edward Crosby (New York) and William Jones (Baltimore) McCurdy Papers, AO.

[30] *The Missionary Messenger*, September 1, 1875.

[31] This AME Church was founded by Blacks in 1840. Hill, "Negroes in Toronto," 78.

[32] Grant 45. Also Westfall 68. During the 1850s, the Canadian Wesleyan Methodist New Connexion Missionary Society experienced rejuvenated growth, as new chapels were built, debts removed and home missions cultivated.

[33] Simpson 250.

[34] *Provincial Freeman*, November 10, 1855.

[35] Howe 59. For more on self-reliance of Blacks in Windsor see *Tri-Weekly Globe*, November 27, 1852.

[36] *St. Thomas Times Journal*, July 22, 1973.

[37] Minutes of the First Baptist Church, Sandwich, Windsor, March 4, 1852, June 17, 1852. CBA.

[38] Minutes of the First Baptist Church, Sandwich, December 8, 1851. CBA.

[39] Minutes of the First Baptist Church, Sandwich, November 1856, September 3, 1859.

[40] Minutes of the First Baptist Church, Sandwich, September 3, 1859, January 1861, June 30, 1866, April 6, 1867, November 30, 1867. CBA.

[41] One illustration is the founding of the First Baptist Church at North Buxton. On July 4, 1853, Geo. Hutter and his wife Mary Ann gave a portion of Lot 6 concession 11 to members of the First Baptist Church, North Buxton. The trustees were Isaac Washington, Alfred West and Wm. A. Jackson.

[42] Bishop Nazrey's address in Proceedings of the Thirteenth session of the Annual Conference of the British Methodist Episcopal Church of the Dominion of Canada,14. UCA.

[43] See Minutes of the First Baptist Church, Sandwich, November 10, 1855, December 8, 1855. CBA.

[44] Bishop Nazrey's address in Proceedings of the Thirteenth session of the Annual Conference of the British Methodist Episcopal Church of the Dominion of Canada, 5.

[45] Steward 300.

[46] Proceedings of the Chatham Convention May 25, 1869, 19.

[47] Proceedings of the Chatham Convention May 25, 1869, 22

[48] Correspondence between Bishop Nazrey and the Executors of Charles Avery's will. 16-17. UCA.

[49] See Cheryl Sanders, "Slavery and Conversion: An Analysis of Ex-slave Testimony" (PhD diss., Harvard University, 1985).

[50] See Patrick Bascio, "Black Theology: Its Critique of Classical or Scholastic Theology" (PhD diss., Fordham University, New York, 1987).

[51] James H. Cone, "The Sources and Norm of Black Theology," in *The Black Experience in Religion*, ed. C. Eric Lincoln, 114 (New York: Anchor Press, 1974).

[52] See Terrie Aamodt, "Righteous Armies, Holy Cause Apocalyptic Images and the Civil War" (PhD diss., Boston University, 1987).

[53] Thomson 47.

[54] Winks, *Blacks in Canada*, 337.

[55] Winks, *Blacks in Canada*, 339.

[56] Winks, *Blacks in Canada*, 337.

[57] Peter J. Paris, "The Spirituality of African Peoples," *Dalhousie Review* 73 (1973): 296.

[58] Bobby Neeley, "Contemporary Afro-American Voodooism: The retention and Adaptation of the Ancient African-Egyptian Mystery System" (PhD diss., University of California, Berkeley, 1988).

[59] See Willie Coleman, "A Study of African American Slave Narratives as a Source for a Contemporary, Constructive Black Theology" (PhD diss., Graduate Theological Union, 1993).

[60] See Preston Washington, "The Black Religious Imagination: A Theological and a Pedagogical Interpretation of the Afro-American Sermon in the Twentieth Century" (PhD diss., Columbia University Teachers College, 1991).

[61] See Amy Young, "Risk and Material Conditions of American-American Slaves at Locust Grove: An Archaeological Perspective," (PhD diss., University of Tennessee, 1995).

[62] *Autobiography of King* 87.

[63] See David E. Goatley, *Were You There? Godforsakeness in Slave Religion* (New York: Orbis Books, 1996), 44. James H. Cone, *The Spirituals and the Blues: An interpretation.* (New York: Seabury Press, 1972), 34.

[64] Jon M. Spencer. "The Rhythms of Black Folks," in *Ain't gonna lay my 'ligion down*, 45.

[65] Wright, *African Americans in the Colonial Era*, 98.

[66] Blassingame 134.

[67] Shreve 42.

[68] See Paul McIntyre, *Black Pentecostal Music in Windsor* (Ottawa: National Museum of Canada, 1976).

[69] Roger 408.

[70] See Mark Hyman, "Afrocentric Leanings of Black Church-Owned Newspapers from mid-nineteenth Century to WW1" (PhD diss., Temple University, 1992).

CHAPTER SIX

THE LAST SUPPER:
SUPERFICIAL ASSIMILATION OF BLACKS

Because the Israelites are my servants, whom I brought out of Egypt, they must not be sold as slaves. Do not rule over them ruthlessly, but fear your God. (Leviticus 25: 42-43)

Religion in the United States aided Blacks in assimilating into Canadian society. An illustration is the moral conduct of the enslaved in Georgia. Their world comprised expectation for character and conduct which were entrenched in social institutions as religion and family.[1] There was a considerable degree of assimilation as the enslaved faked adherence to the teachings of the planter. During most of the nineteenth century in Chicago, Protestants adhered to certain virtues as diligence, self-control and temperance. The cultural dominance of Protestants led to formulation of a self-identity. This was the behaviour expected from immigrants and the formerly enslaved.[2]

Some churches in Canada played a pivotal role in reinforcing religious mores in allowing a better chance of appreciating bi-racial education, handling demands of leadership and being better suited for assimilation. By producing Blacks who were morally and ethically upright, the process of assimilation would be easier as religion became the "opium of the masses." By 1860, the AMA's accounts provided evidence that the fugitives in Canada were industrious, enterprising and moral.[3] The role of the church in assimilation was a paradoxical one because even though it promoted assimilation through education and the development of Black leaders it was guilty of segregation with its all-Black settlements, separate pews and burial plots. Nevertheless, these discriminatory practices were not a setback to the Blacks adhering to the Protestant denominations.

An examination of the assimilation and segregation of Blacks in Canada revealed racism and prejudice being causal factors in the division of congregations and the eventual creation of separate schools and churches. One of the reasons the Black Methodists in Upper Canada embraced the AME in the 1830s was due to the hostile and cold reception meted out by the White Methodist churches.[4] The solution to this dilemma was certainly not confined to the mission but was present in the everyday experiences of Blacks. John Farrell argued that since their arrival in Canada Blacks were disadvantaged in Upper Canada and believed that most of this prejudice emanated from the lower White class.[5] This is ironic because in the United States, "Worship often was with the lower-class Whites."[6] The many obstacles faced by Blacks in Canada reinforced the belief that discrimination in Canada was as strong and persistent as in the United States.[7]

In Nova Scotia, Blacks were eager to be integrated in the schools and churches which were populated by Whites. However, this integration failed and Blacks were unable to build separate institutions. White philanthropic groups and church organisations willingly responded and provided the necessary funding and material for Blacks to establish their institutions.[8] By the mid-1780s, the emergence of independent all-Black churches was the result of "an unChristian white racial exclusiveness."[9]

Indeed, after the passage of the Fugitive Slave Act in the United States in 1850, the increase of Blacks in Canada contributed to the corresponding surge in racial tension.[10] Probably some Whites in Canada would have been concerned that these Blacks would be a burden on the social services and/or become involved in anti-social activities such as crime. Despite the few negative public responses, Fred Landon, a researcher on Blacks in Canada, argued, "In general the Black people were received with kindness and efforts were made to assist them in their chief needs."[11] Supporting this viewpoint is Daniel Hill's contention that in Toronto, a cordial relationship existed between the two ethnicities, and that after passage of the Fugitive Slave Act, "The new arrivals did not hinder the integration and absorption of Negroes into the schools, religious and other institutions in the city."[12] As late as 1853, the second Annual Report of the Anti-Slavery Society of Canada confirmed incidents of prejudice against the coloured population and emphasised, "instances in the Western District and along the frontier, where a strong and unchristian prejudice against Negroes still prevails, even in the case of some Christian professors."[13]

One of the visible indicators of assimilation attempts was the widespread involvement of White Protestant leaders and members in secular, humanitarian organisations. They sought the improvement of the refugees and free Blacks in Upper Canada/Canada West. After the passage of the Fugitive Slave Act the influx of Blacks to Canada demanded increased efforts among existing societies which led to the formation of a

Canadian based anti-slavery organisation. In February 1851 Rev. William McClure, a White Presbyterian minister, met with interested persons at Toronto to formulate plans for a vibrant anti-slavery group to pressure the United States into freeing the enslaved. Also, Rev. Michael Willis, an advocate of anti-slavery, faithfully served as president of the Anti-Slavery Society of Canada.[14] The involvement of these prominent White persons in the anti-slavery movement contributed to the gradual undermining of slavery in the United States.

Assistance of Women and Groups

The duty of monitoring the morals and welfare of the Blacks was not the burden of the Protestant churches in Canada. Instead, a host of secular societies had arisen and shared the task of assisting the social interactions of the formerly enslaved and overseeing their material needs. These fraternal and benevolent organisations adhered to the belief of racial solidarity among Black churches.[15] Most of these organisations worked closely with the Protestant faiths and possessed a common agenda to uplift and assist the coloured settlers. The Amherstburg True Band Society (founded in 1854) assisted in the settling of slaves in Upper Canada and its success at Amherstburg hastened the spread of the group's work to other Black settlements.[16] This society comprised mostly coloured members and adhered to Christian values. The group sought to reduce interdenominational divisions as a result of doctrinal teachings, to encourage school attendance of Blacks and campaign for an improved education system.[17] Such objectives and external support from these groups directly contributed to the survival and stability of the Black settlements.

The spiritual and temporal welfare of the free Black population was not a domain exclusive of women. During the first half of the nineteenth century, White and Black women made substantial contributions in alleviating the plight of the refugees in Canada. In 1825, a women's group made and distributed clothes to needy Blacks residing in Preston and Hammonds Plains in Nova Scotia.[18] Groups such as The Toronto Ladies' Association for the Relief of Destitute Coloured Fugitives and the West London Ladies' Association, a Canadian mission branch of the Colonial Church and School Society were dominated by sympathetic Whites. Likewise, in the town of Cobourg, women interested in eradicating slavery banded together to form a Ladies Association for promoting the Christian mission among Blacks.[19] In 1854, Chatham's Black wives founded the Victoria Reform Benevolent Society to assist needy women.[20] However, it is unfortunate that the existing primary sources do not provide more information on the pivotal role of women amongst the fugitives.

During 1837-1847, White women in Illinois publicly expressed support for the rights of Blacks including the enslaved and fugitive free Blacks. However, men sought to abruptly curtail this freedom of expression.[21] From the 1820s, the vocal female abolitionists in Britain added to the international movement to end slavery.[22] Contacts between female activists in the United States and Britain ensured a successful anti-slavery campaign. This social reform of the nineteenth century was vital as women were perceived by the society as being morally superior to men and as protectors of the purity of society and the family.

The prejudiced treatment in Upper Canada was also experienced in the United States and Nova Scotia. Whites in Tuscaloosa County in Alabama and Washtenaw County in Michigan felt the elimination of major social problems could be achieved by preaching benevolence and temperance to the free population. As a result, the Blacks were often the willing recipients of White benevolence.[23] Donald Clairmont and Dennis Magill in *Nova Scotian Blacks* argued that many Blacks initially sought integration with Whites in schools and churches. The failure of these attempts led many Blacks to consider building separate structures but they were unable to afford the costs. This was eventually achieved due to the financial assistance of White groups.[24]

In Canada, Henson, a Methodist preacher from the United States, had a small band of religious followers and they decided to grow wheat and tobacco on lands they rented near Colchester. Henson realised the importance of education and lands for the progress of displaced Blacks. By 1834, Henson began searching for a site and opted to establish the all-Black Dawn Settlement in Kent County on land near the town of Dresden in the province of Ontario. In 1836, he met and received assistance from a Congregationalist missionary, Rev. Hiram Wilson of Massachusetts, who was well-known among anti-slavery groups in the United States.

Two hundred acres of land were purchased by James Fuller, a Quaker from New York, in 1841. In this year, the Dawn Settlement and a manual training school- the British American Institute were organised. A year after being established, twelve students enrolled at the Institute to learn various trades. The Institute was funded primarily by donations and operated by an Executive Committee and a Board of Trustees. Those attending were required to pay the necessary fees. The Dawn Settlement of 500 persons on 1,500 acres gradually expanded and the self-sustaining community, grew corn, tobacco, oats and wheat.[25] They also possessed a brickyard, grist and saw mills.

The founding principles of the philanthropic organisations in Canada were akin to the mission of the Protestant Church as they sought to inculcate morals in Blacks. As early as 1840, part of the ongoing effort to improve the education among Blacks and elevate their status, involved a petition submitted by individuals in London to establish a company to be incorporated as the "Wilberforce Benevolent School Company of Upper Canada."[26] Also expressing concerns was the Wilberforce Lyceum Educating Society at Cannonsburg in Colchester:

> ...in order to sustain a moral and enlightened position for ourselves and those that have religious ambitions to join us, have as rule subjects established this institution for the promotion of the rising generation in education...as will promote the furtberance of the true religion of God...."[27]

The ethos of such a group was to project an image of progress and stability that would attract Blacks.

The promotion of independence among Black communities did not impede the contribution of Blacks to the churches. The role of the churches in the Black communities served to make Christianity a useful reality in their lives. Physical contributions in the form of labour by the Black settlers ensured the maintenance and building of many a church and school. In Sharon Roger's analysis of the Blacks in Buxton she argued, "The settlement's original objectives did not, after all, include wealth. They did include improvement and self-reliance."[28] And, this striving for self-reliance is clearly illustrated in such activities as reaping crops and constructing homes. Additionally, Howard Law identified the agricultural success of the homesteading plan as an indicator of Buxton's quest for self-reliance.[29] This idea was adopted by Rev. Foote, a leader overseeing the Refugee Home Society. He stressed that the goals included industry and self-dependence.[30] S.G. Howe provided an account of a thanksgiving service on the completion of a Black Methodist church with an atmosphere of the euphoria marking the historic occasion:

> The building of the church had been a long and painful business. They had been much perplexed about the ways and means, and each one had exerted himself to the utmost....One after another got up and spoke simply and earnestly, but very forcibly; and everyone congratulated himself upon having been humbly instrumental....[31]

It should not be assumed that the survival of these settlements was a solo effort on the part of Blacks because the philanthropic efforts of individuals and institutions ensured these settlements would progress.

Support from external sources would have enabled Blacks to focus their energies on expanding their missionary efforts. One of the paradoxes of these religious-based settlements was that though they offered psychological support and emotional protection, there was the inevitable physical isolation which worked against the forces of acculturation and assimilation.

In 1854, one of the self-help strategies of the Buxton mission was a bazaar to raise funds to assist the less fortunate in the settlement.[32] In Buxton's schools, those students who could not afford to pay the required small sum of money were granted free education.[33] By the end of 1866, this benevolent gesture was expanded as settlers were voluntarily taxed for the support of the four schools.[34] It was King's dream to discard the attitude of depending upon the paternalism of Whites for survival. He envisioned a spirit of independence which would offer financial freedom for the Blacks. Furthermore, this economic independence sent a message in removing stereotypes as Blacks were sometimes embarrassed that their attempts at raising funds would be perceived as begging by the Whites.[35] In an effort to reduce the negative image, King also established a local, all-Black arbitration court to deal with internal problems of the settlement.[36]

A similar concern was expressed in the act of incorporation of the Elgin Settlement in 1850 with one of its objectives being the "moral improvement of the Coloured Population."[37] The Fugitives' Union and the Windsor Anti-Slavery Society were small-scale efforts which were instrumental in serving the needs of recently displaced refugees.[38] Undoubtedly, these societies in Canada West helped foster a spirit of obedience and created role models for the Black communities. Such service-oriented efforts were proof of the paternalistic role and influence from groups operating outside the realm of the church. These groups displayed Christian virtues of caring and concern.

Some efforts met with resistance from Blacks. For instance, in 1859 an effort was made to establish a group for "the elevation and education of the Colored People of Canada." Whilst the legislation was being debated in the Canadian Parliament, Blacks in Canada held protests against the colour distinction. The *Douglass Monthly*, a pro-Black newspaper based in the United States, believed the protests were justified:

> This is one of the most sensible protests in which the colored people of Canada ever united. If the White people of Canada as well as the White people of the United States would only be just with the Negro they would not have much occasion to be generous to him....special and partial legislation of colored people degrades them in the eyes of the whites, weakens their own self-respect, destroys their self-reliance, leaves them to

look for favors rather than rights, induces servility instead of manly independence and divests them of that firmness of character which is essential to a successful career on the part of an individual or a race.[39]

Despite assistance to Canada some concerns were expressed. In 1859 the African Aid Society based in the United States voiced its concerns over the exploitation of fugitive Blacks in Canada. The society requested measures to, "...prevent the swarms of professional beggars who go through the country soliciting aid for fugitives which the fugitive seldom gets." Furthermore, the group claimed, "Nobody seems to know what really becomes of the money and clothing collected by different individuals."[40] Similarly in December 1864, the *British Constitution* of Fergus reported the presence on the streets of three orphan Black girls who were almost naked, and badly affected by the weather.[41] The lack of transparency and accountability affected the public's perception of humanitarian initiatives.

Voluntary groups performed similar tasks, as the church, in providing education and material needs for the fugitives. Their existence and discipline was the nursery for future Black leaders. In Upper Canada there were fourteen such organisations intent on fostering an independent spirit among the colored settlements.[42] The Refugee Home Society and Refugee Slaves' Friend Society were organizations catering specifically to the needs of Blacks. One scholar argued that the Refugee Home Society aided the former enslaved persons in the adjustment to their free and independent status and provided hundreds of fugitives with clothing and shelter upon their arrival in Canada.[43] The Society's goals were strikingly similar to those espoused by Protestant missions as the former provided land, education and banned the intake of alcohol on its settlement. For instance, Article 2 of the Society stated, "The object of the society shall be to obtain permanent homes for the Refugees in Canada, and to promote their moral, social, physical intellectual and political elevation."[44] A strong religious influence within the Refugee Home Society was evident in 1857 with the choice of Rev. Kitchell as a committee member to report on its progress.[45] Alexander Murray argued that these efforts generated an anti-slavery impulse in Canada with a unique religious base.[46] Such anti-slavery objectives with strong religious overtones complimented the churches which were busily working to imbue desirable qualities in the fugitives. There were some exceptions. For instance, the founder of the Black Baptist Church in the Maritimes was David George who was a Baptist minister from South Carolina. He was able establish the churches in Canada without philanthropic assistance from Whites.[47]

A sense of harmony prevailed among the social service organisations, philanthropic individuals and Protestant churches. The spirit of goodwill endured and the churches appreciated any assistance to the fugitive Blacks. These voluntary groups were able to work alongside the missions in the same communities without petty jealousies. In this regard these societies exemplified the Christian virtues of charity and benevolence. More importantly, the presence of Whites and Blacks in these societies was an indicator of tolerance at the community level in Canada. Without these Christian-oriented organisations providing education and material services, the Protestant church might have been forced to double its missionary efforts. The churches, mission schools and secular groups satisfied physical and material needs whilst offering emotional support to the coloured population. The integrated classes at the mission schools served an important role in the assimilation and acculturation of Blacks.

Emigration and Shortcomings of the White Church

The emigration schemes, designed to relocate the Blacks in Canada, were an indication of the Church's shortcomings in dealing with the eradication or reduction of discrimination in the eighteenth and nineteenth centuries. A proposed solution to the dilemma of segregation in Canadian society was relocation to lands in which the Blacks would be removed from injustices and in a more hospitable environment.

One Nova Scotian Black who served as a sergeant in the "Black Pioneers" was Thomas Peters. He initially resided at Annapolis and later applied for land in New Brunswick. His application was rejected and he decided to complain to the Secretary of State for the Colonies, Lord Grenville. This soon led to an investigation of the situation of free Blacks, and Peters also expressed his desire to migrate to a country with a warmer climate. Fortunately, the Sierra Leone Company indicated their interest in relocating the Blacks who desired to leave Nova Scotia. On 15 January 1792 there was the emigration of 1,192 Blacks who boarded 15 ships and departed Halifax Harbour for Sierra Leone in Africa. This action was undertaken by Blacks after "broken promises of land and social emancipation."[48] These Blacks had been temporarily residing in Preston, Halifax, Saint John and Digby with a total of 222 from New Brunswick.[49] Among the passengers were members of Moses Wilkinson's Methodist congregation, Lady Huntington's Connection and the rest were Baptists.[50] Most of the school teachers and religious teachers joined the group and along with David George established the first Baptist Church in West Africa. Lamin Sanneh in *West African Christianity* described this effort as possessing elements of "religious idealism and the dream of an African Utopia."[51]

In judging the role of religion in the assimilation of Blacks in Canada there needs to be an appreciation of their previous religious experiences. In the United States, White churches tended to promote segregation as many Blacks were either denied religious instruction or exposed to distorted versions of Christianity. Thus, for some Blacks in the United States, Protestantism was increasingly identified with oppression and meant limited freedom. In Canada the Blacks were able to openly embrace Christianity. In the United States, the main underpinning of the Blacks' religion was a desire for change in their circumstances and belief in the eventual punishment for cruel, unjust planters.[52]

In documenting the Black experience in Canada there is the tendency among some researchers to downplay the contributions of Whites.[53] Often the early assimilation among some of the waves of Blacks to Canada can be traced to their early contacts with the White clergy who temporarily sheltered them after the traumatic ordeal of the Underground Railroad.[54] In the settlements and schools the contact with Protestant missions, headed by Whites was instrumental in satisfying the material needs of the Blacks. Furthermore, sometimes White philanthropic individuals and groups, from Canada and abroad, provided financial support throughout the life of most settlements. Thus, in analysing the relationship forged between Blacks and religion the assistance of sympathetic Whites cannot be underestimated or obscured by sporadic acts of discrimination in Canada.

It would be easy to assume that slavery's end and the return of some Blacks to the United States was a direct result of their failure to assimilate in Canada. Robin Winks contended, "Fugitive slaves were harboured in the provinces but on the whole not accepted. Most Maritimers were spectators, not participants, in the abolitionist crusade."[55] This would have contributed to the Blacks feeling as strangers and desiring to again cross the border. In the aftermath of the Civil War (1861-1865) there was a noticeable decrease among some Canadian Black communities as thousands returned to the United States.[56] At this time, the Black population of Canada West was an estimated 11,000 persons. Almost 60% of Blacks in Canada West returned to the United States when the Northern states were victorious over the Southern states in 1865.[57]

Blacks in Canada remembered friends and relatives and also the end of the dreaded slavery era. In August 1863, at Hawkesville, there was a gathering of Blacks from Wellesley and Peel Townships to commemorate the emancipation of the formerly enslaved.[58] During the 1870s, Blacks in Chatham stopped observing 1 August as Emancipation Day because "they were not accorded freedom and justice." They claimed good treatment in Detroit and Windsor but in Chatham only one hotel and restaurant would allow Blacks.[59] Furthermore, Blacks in the counties of Lincoln, Kent and Essex met to discuss such issues as their denial of educational opportunities at public schools and rejection from jury duty. Such blatant infringements on liberties certainly prompted Blacks to consider returning to the United States.

Undoubtedly, the prejudice experienced by Blacks was a determining factor in their decision to return to the United States. For instance Austin Steward, formerly of Rochester, New York, who later resided in London (in Canada West), published his views of the decision to leave Canada:

> ...and although they had willingly accompanied me to Canada, where they had experienced little less than care, labor and sorrow, it cannot be thought very strange that they should desire to return. We were colored people to be sure, and were too often made to feel the weight of that cruel prejudice, which small minds with a perverted education, know so well how to heap upon the best endeavours of our oppressed race."[60]

The status of Blacks as sojourners in Canada was not unforeseen because despite the horrors of slavery, the feelings of homesickness persisted and the longing for family and friends gnawed at their minds. The decision of Blacks to return to the United States was not necessarily due to discrimination but typical of any immigrant who is involuntarily separated from loved ones.[61] After slavery ended, Blacks, born in the United States and residing in Canada, were more inclined to return to the United States. Canadian-born Blacks and those who had lost contact with relatives in the United States were more likely to remain in Canada. Thus, it is difficult to use statistics of return migration in determining the success or failure of the assimilation process. The decrease in the Black population in certain areas of Canada West cannot be attributed solely to migration to the United States. For instance, during the 1870s, Blacks in North Buxton settled in other parts of the province.[62]

The shortcomings of the White church in promoting assimilation amongst Blacks did not seem to be a major reason for the return of Blacks to the United States. Before slavery was abolished the superficial nature of assimilation was apparent, "That they have not taken firm root in Canada and that they earnestly desire to go to the southern region of the United States, partly from love of warmth, but more from love of *home*."[63] Nonetheless, during their stay in Canada, Blacks seemed to have accepted both Canada and the United States as home and this double-consciousness or 'dual-homeland' concept was strikingly similar to the Italian immigrant's two loyalties (chiaroscuro) in which home was considered both Toronto and the village or town in Italy.[64] Blacks were not fleeing Canada because of inadequate churches, leaders or discrimination but, as Donald Simpson argued, to be reunited with family and friends.[65] Thus the return to the United States cannot be explained solely in terms of the segregation in schools and churches in Canada.

During slavery, with little hope of being reunited with families, Blacks seemed to accept their fate in Canada and assimilation seemed inevitable. However, the removal of the harsh sentence of slavery meant that years of work by the White churches in Upper Canada would be undermined. In 1865, Bishop Nazrey issued a warning to those interested in returning, by drawing reference to the ill-fated Haitian colonisation scheme. The steady loss of members was inevitable and as certain ministers of the BME Church departed they were followed by faithful members.[66] The great challenge for the Protestant denominations, which once had a vibrant Black following, was to convince its membership of the futility in returning to the United States to rebuild their lives.

Upon slavery's demise in 1865, the United States became appealing to Blacks and this seemed to override their time and effort in maintaining the religious-based communities in Canada. Indeed, with the Emancipation Proclamation in 1863, the exodus of Blacks to the United States was a crucial blow to the assimilation efforts undertaken by the White and Black churches in Canada West. In the post-1865 period, with the passage of the Fourteenth and Fifteen Amendments and the First and Second Reconstruction Acts, in the United States, the stage was set for many Blacks to return to family and friends.[67] Under such protective legislation, there were visible indicators of reform and Blacks were optimistic they would be empowered with citizenship and voting rights. This atmosphere of freedom and transformation was an impetus for a steady flow of Blacks from Canadian churches to abandon their settlements and return southward. However there was a considerable number of Blacks in urban areas in Ontario by 1871 (see Table 6-1).

Table 6-1: Population of urban areas in Ontario

Urban areas	Total population	Black population	Black% of total
Windsor	4,253	874	20.5
Amherstburg	1,936	301	15.5
St. Catherines	7,864	481	6.1
London	15,826	330	2.0
Niagara	1,600	31	1.9
Hamilton	26,716	350	1.3
Toronto	56,092	551	0.9
Peterborough	4,611	5	0.1

(Source: Jonathan Walton, "Blacks in Buxton and Chatham 1830-1890: Did the 49th Parallel Make a Difference?" PhD diss., Princeton University, 1979, 317.)

After 1865, the Canadian churches with a significant Black membership, increasingly felt powerless to curb the tide of return migration. The consequence of this exodus had a negative impact on the churches. Catherine Brooks contended that after the Civil War, Buxton's church property depreciated and ministers were unable to earn a salary.[68] Likewise, in 1876, elders of the St. Andrews Church reported prayer meetings were uncharacteristically poorly attended.[69] It seemed strange that after the Black population had laboured in erecting churches and schools, invested time and energy in the training of leaders and teachers, they would suddenly depart for the United States. Interestingly, there is no evidence that after the Emancipation Proclamation, some freed families opted to join the established communities in Canada West. Obviously, this departure for the United States questioned the apparent success of integration of Blacks in Canada.

Some White leaders and their congregations seemed to be influenced by the prevailing anti-Black sentiment in Upper Canada. The AMA in its Report of 1853 chose to highlight the increased opposition to White missionaries as a result of the misrepresentation of coloured preachers.[70] In another instance, the members of the Black community in London believed that racial prejudice stemmed from the United States.[71] It was difficult to quell the prevailing phobia of Blacks in Canada during the nineteenth century. On learning of the intentions of the Rev. King to introduce Blacks in Raleigh, the *Chatham Journal* vehemently argued against such a preposterous suggestion which would fail to produce any benefits.[72] A similar stance was taken at a public meeting in Chatham in which opposition voices condemned the scheme proposed by the Elgin Association for settling the Township of Raleigh with Blacks. In a public address by a disgruntled resident, concerns were expressed over the thousands of American Blacks entering Canada which resulted in "...their poisonous effect upon the moral and social habits of a community."[73] The severely limited options of Blacks explain their inability to protest against these prejudices of the residents. The reaction of Whites was not wholly unfounded. There were isolated incidents which reflected badly on Blacks. An article entitled "A Darkey in Trouble" in the *Elora Observer* reported on a drunken Black who was always a nuisance and had his house torn down.[74] Also, two Blacks were arrested for stealing a goose in Elora and were referred to as "scamps."[75]

There is little evidence that the Protestant churches in Canada seemed overwhelmed or publicly responded to these racially motivated outbursts. However, some of the White religious leaders were determined to continue working among the Blacks which averted increased polarisation of the ethnic groups. In the midst of intense opposition, the stance by the churches to continue in Black settlements left an indelible impression and made Blacks more religious.

Favouring the Chosen Ones: Segregation

In Florida, in White-controlled and racially mixed churches, Blacks were relegated to special galleries and pews.[76] Likewise, in Georgia racially mixed Baptist churches offered insignificant spiritual equality.[77] These shortcomings contributed to Blacks establishing their churches and appealing for Black ministers in the post-1865 era. For instance, during the late 1870s in Wilkes County, Georgia, Blacks departed biracial churches and formed separate religious institutions.[78] To avoid segregation in the Moravian Church in North Carolina, by 1822 Blacks opted to organise all-Black congregations who were led by a White minister.[79] This separation would have positive benefits on Blacks since "...the more closely blacks worshipped with whites, the less they wanted to become Christians."[80]

Indeed, it seemed contradictory that White preachers condemned the oppressive slavery system yet allowed discrimination within the Canadian churches. This has been one of the major contradictions of the mission in Canada. Blacks were not the only ethnic group to experience this segregation, a similar situation arose in the Methodist mission in Chatham which had two churches, one serving Whites and the other designated for native Indians.[81] One of the obvious reasons the Blacks tolerated segregated congregations was their small numbers in comparison to the larger White population. This would account for the relatively weak, Black opposition to this discrimination. There was the double disadvantage of being a non-White minority group and also being a refugee.[82] Thus their survival strategies seemed to be ignoring the problem of discrimination because they were thankful and grateful for escaping slavery. Whilst enslaved in the United States, the self-conceptualised response of many was to accept the here and now but not the system of slavery.[83] Prior to 1830, even though some of the White Protestant Canadian missions appeared hypocritical as their practices contradicted with their Biblical teachings, there was no alternative worship available to Blacks.

It can be argued that the discrimination existing in the churches was an extension of society's deplorable treatment of Blacks in Canada:

> Acts of discrimination, such as the denial of accommodation on steam-boats and stage-coaches, and in hotels, led to the formation of numerous self-help organizations and the establishment of all-black churches, which became the cultural as well as spiritual, focal points of the communities.[84]

Undoubtedly, the segregation of Blacks in churches was one of the fundamental reasons for the emergence of separate Black churches and leaders. Peter Paris in *The Moral, Political and Religious Significance of the Black Churches in Nova Scotia* argued that the emergence of separate Black churches were an alternative to the racist secular and religious White institutions.[85]

Inevitably, racism during slavery had repercussions on the churches in the United States. Additionally, the formation of Detroit's Black community in 1836 occurred when 13 Blacks resigned from the First Baptist Church and formed the Society of Second Baptist Church.[86] During 1832 to 1852, the enslaved and free Blacks of Court Street Methodist Church in Montgomery were forced to sit in galleries during Sunday services.[87]

In Nova Scotia there were Whites who seemed sympathetic to the plight of the Blacks and condemned slavery, yet allowed unequal treatment in their churches by prohibiting Blacks from certain pews. At Anglican services, Blacks were seated separately in the balconies. Furthermore, by 1784 there was a special gallery for Blacks during worship services at St. Paul's Church.[88] During the 1780s, some Methodist churches restricted Blacks to special galleries, and those Blacks, who were members of the Church of England in Halifax, formed separate congregations.[89] Likewise, in 1815 a Roman Catholic priest identified a problem existing among Blacks in a church at Tracadie:

> There is a complaint that these newcomers bring in a bad odour, and that there is no way to put up with them, because of the shortage of space in our

little chapel. A sure way to bring about peace would be to construct a gallery where the blacks alone would be admitted.[90]

The relegation to separation pews was the initial phase and subsequently Blacks in Nova Scotia were advised to desist from attending Sunday services with Whites and thus Blacks held separate services led by Black lay-readers.[91]

In some Upper Canadian churches, Whites derogatorily referred to the separate pews as "Nigger Heaven" and there were also special galleries for Blacks.[92] But this physical separation did not seem to have an adverse effect on the spirituality of Blacks or a profound impact on Black theology. The separation of Blacks and eventual formation of their churches was partly a result of discrimination and the segregated form of worship seemed to have a deleterious effect:

> That when they congregate in large numbers in one locality; and establish separate churches and schools, they not only excite prejudices of race in others, but develop a spirit of caste among themselves, and make less progress than where they form a small part of the local population.[93]

The segregation of Blacks was an ominous cloud which obscured future substantial victories in education and leadership.

Acts of discrimination against Blacks led to a questioning of the intentions of White religious leaders. Even in death, the burial of church members was met by the icy hand of prejudice as illustrated in the journal of Rev. Dillon, pastor at Chatham, who provided evidence of segregated burials.[94] Furthermore, the burial plots at Amherstburg, Windsor, Puce and Colchester and the BME Cemetery were specifically allocated for Blacks. Such cemeteries were Rose Hill at Town Line in Amherstburg and the Negro Cemetery on the northside of Highway 2 near Puce Road in Windsor Grove. Other cemeteries for Blacks were located at Yatton (four miles northwest of Elmira). In the Normanby Township there is a designated area (lot 50, concession 3) as the burial ground of Blacks, similar areas existed in Queen's Bush settlement (in the area north and west of Berlin, present-day Kitchener and Guelph in the direction of the lakes), Peel Township and Oxford County.[95] In the official registers of Québec there is a site known as "Nigger Rock" where slaves were buried. These Blacks would have been buried during the 1800s and archival records mention the "St. Armand Negro Burying Ground."[96]

Segregated graveyards were an extension of the separate schools and churches which were a norm in Canada. The segregated burials provide blatant evidence that White Protestants seemed to have sanctioned a practice of separation from pews to coffins and thus consciously created barriers for Blacks during the nineteenth century. Segregation was not confined to the churches as the old Durham Road Pioneer Cemetery located in Artemesia Township, Grey County was the final resting place for Loyalists of African descent.[97] At the site are four broken tombstones with dates from 1854 to 1863.

These deliberate measures deepened the schism between Blacks and Whites. The implementation of discriminatory practices and the desire of Blacks to leave Canada certainly shed new light on the sincerity of Whites. The repercussion of segregation on the Black Church was inevitable:

> ...for as whites denied Negroes access to the pulpit and to the priesthood, black men blazed their own segregated paths toward high office. These leaders and the churches they led came to accept segregation, to encourage the idea of racial solidarity, and to provide one means for social accommodation between the races...they also developed a black Christ.[98]

The relations between the two ethnicities did not always hinge on hostility and it is believed that until 1850 satisfactory Black-White relations existed.[99] There were exceptions to the discriminatory treatment such as demonstrated by Birney, a United States visitor to Toronto, who attended the English (Episcopal) Church and witnessed coloured people seated together with Whites. He also attended a Baptist Church with its spiritual leader being Christian, a former enslaved Virginian, and the congregation having an equal number of Blacks and Whites, "There was no distinction in seats, nor any, the least recognition, so far as I could discern, of a difference made by complexion or any other cause."[100]

In the postbellum era in the United States, there was a mixed response of Whites to the splintering of their congregations and formation of separate Black churches. During the 1880s, Blacks at the First Presbyterian Church in Montgomery, Alabama requested a separate church and a Black preacher. The White members provided finances for the First Colored Church and allowed a Black minister.[101] The development of Black churches might have been misinterpreted and frowned upon by White religious leaders as a sign of ungratefulness or rebelliousness. An illustration is the Southern Presbyterians, who were displeased that Black congregations felt "freed from white guidance and discipline."[102] Such a move would have been welcomed by other Whites due to the fact that:

> ...most congregations would appear to have preferred that Negroes worship elsewhere, and not necessarily for reasons of ethnicity. The newly arrived

Negroes were socially less adept, they enjoyed a more enthusiastic sermon and song, and sometimes they seemed doctrinally sound.[103]

In retrospect, the decision of Blacks to secede from White churches was due to doctrinal differences, overcrowding, convenience and personality conflicts.[104]

During the 1820s and 1830s, there were interracial Black Baptist churches located at Niagara, Colchester and Toronto. By the early 1840s, this changed as fugitive Blacks sought "to restrict membership to blacks lest the pharoahs from whom they had fled infiltrate them."[105] Indeed, Black churches provided a basic need for the Blacks- protection from the "hostility of a racist social order."[106] From 1834 to 1835, Rev. Slight initially admired the Black population in Amherstburg but as the Blacks began organising their churches, his views changed as the Wesleyan missionary noted with dismay, "We have endeavoured to keep up means of grace, especially devoted to the Coloured people; but arising from their former habits, they are the most fickle and unstable people I have ever met."[107] This viewpoint encapsulates an underlying sense of failure of the mission arising from the loss of its Black members. A similar development unfolded in the Coloured Wesleyan Methodist Church as Blacks sought to break ties with the parent church. After separation, the church comprised only 8-10 regular members and did not benefit from the services of a regularly ordained minister.[108] In response to this request, Rev. Wilkinson leader of the Wesleyan Church mobilised a second Wesleyan body and approved a new board of trustees to act as the presiding elder of the Coloured Wesleyan Methodists. But by 1855 another sour relationship appeared on the horizon, as Rev. W. Boulder, who replaced Rev. Wilkinson, became leader of the White Wesleyans and attempted to reclaim the property (through the new Board of Trustees appointed by Rev. Wilkinson) used by the Coloured Wesleyans. This incident led to embarrassing confrontations and was finally settled in court in favour of the Coloured Wesleyans who continued to actively worship till 1875.

It was unfortunate that the desire of Blacks seeking religious independence was seen as insubordination by Whites. The brief but turbulent and tragic history of the Coloured Wesleyan Methodist Church appeared uncharacteristic of other Black churches. Its many divisions and battles over property reflect the shortcomings of a predominantly Black denomination which failed to be fully assimilated. The history of this religious group was part of a larger picture of sporadic outbursts of distrust and uncertainty between Blacks and Whites in Canada.

Despite the seemingly negative consequences, Daniel Hill argued that the divisions amongst the churches had unseen benefits, "Internal rifts within the city's Negro churches, together with freedom to worship in any of Toronto's churches, probably had the effect of hurrying the process of integration."[109] Even though contentious issues were often amicably resolved, it is difficult to estimate the untold damage that segregation had on relations between Blacks and Whites. The religious environment which Blacks and Whites operated was frequently tested as the segregation of Blacks and the establishment of separate churches crippled the chances of a cordial relationship developing between the White majority and the Black minority.

It is interesting to note that this transformation occurred among people whose lives on cotton or sugar plantations once revolved around profit maximisation. This economic subculture, without the capitalist influence, can be traced to their escape from the United States with few material possessions and their only concern being freedom. It seemed that in the creation of separate settlements, or those isolated as in Guysborough County in Nova Scotia, Blacks were rebelling against an economic system that uprooted them from Africa. It is unfortunate that though Blacks were successful in constructing churches and maintaining the settlements, they had alienated themselves from the rest of society, thus limiting their integration.

In Canada, the majority of Blacks faced some form of injustice perpetrated by Whites. Individuals as Henson understood the role of the church as protector of the Blacks because he witnessed many instances in which Whites defrauded Blacks.[110] Further disadvantages were endured by those Blacks involved in farming, "their farms were smaller, crop yields per acre lower, and rate of clearing land slower."[111] For example, land in the Oro Township was deemed dry and useless by its residents.[112]

One of the underlying reasons for the failure of the Wilberforce Refugee Colony in Middlesex County, established in 1829, stemmed from ineffective management.[113] Another reason was the refusal of the Canada Land Company to sell more land to the colony due to the fear of discouraging White settlers.[114] As a result the settlement lasted for only six years. This is in contrast to the location of the Elgin Settlement which a Presbyterian committee found to have superior soil, close to markets and a favourable climate.[115] This is debatable since these lands were judged by some as having extensive drainage problems and infertile soil. Nevertheless, the Blacks under the guidance of the Church seemed to have an added advantage over other Blacks in Upper Canada. This isolation inadvertently stunted the religious and social interaction between Blacks and Whites.

The majority of Black churches had not been equipped with the power or ability to transform race relations.[116] In these all-Black communities, the physical separation from Whites mirrored the separation of Black and White churches. One of the paradoxes of the White Protestant churches was their creation and support of all-Black settlements in Canada. The White Protestant churches in the Black communities acted as a stabilising force, a cohesive factor contributing to the longevity of most settlements. Though the concentration of Blacks might have led to close-knit communities, the isolation from other Black settlements and the rest of Canada created obvious obstacles to assimilation. In effect, the churches were guilty of creating pockets of isolated Black settlements.

It is evident that certain aspects of the Protestant mission to Blacks appeared Janus-faced. Religious leaders schooled in the Christian principles of equality and 'love thy neighbour as thyself' seemed to disregard such teachings. Segregated congregations pressured Blacks into seeking separate churches and developing leaders among themselves. There were exceptions such as the St. Andrews Presbyterian Church in Buxton which was integrated. In retrospect, Canada's churches were not entirely at fault, as the pervasive anti-Black sentiment in society provided a justification for segregated worship and education.

Successes of Assimilation

It can be argued that White Protestant churches were not wholly guilty of promoting segregation between the two ethnicities because these all-Black settlements were not unique to the social landscape of Canada. For instance, the Irish tended to congregate in the central areas of Upper Canada and by the end of the nineteenth century, the Italians in Toronto exhibited similar tendencies, as they were clustered in "little Italies." The immigration story is more or less the same- upon the arrival of an ethnic group, the settlers tended to instinctively search for their own kind in the hope of increasing the chances of surviving and adjusting to a new society. But, as the immigrant population increased, this would be accompanied by rising levels of prejudice and racism.

Amidst the reports of discrimination in the churches and schools there were positive accounts of adjustment in the Canadian society. In the Wesleyan mission to Amherstburg, religion seemed to have partially overturned barriers of ethnicity as the worship services at Sandwich proved, "The congregation will consist partly of whites, and partly of coloured people. I was surprised to see 1 Irish and 4 or 5 French Roman

Catholics there" and further evidence of interracial mixing is evident from the special 'Love Feast' which had a favourable attendance of Blacks, Whites and Native Indians.[117] This was a small-scale display of assimilation within the Wesleyan Church, however, it did not last long because the Blacks soon established separate churches in the area.

Outside the shelter of the church, Blacks also seemed to be adjusting. An 1853 Report of the Amherstburg Convention, indicated that members expressed gratitude that this province was hospitable and colour was not an obstacle to the adjustment of Blacks.[118] It can be argued that for Blacks, limited assimilation was able to occur because of a relatively high degree of tolerance in Canada. By adopting the principle of accommodation, Blacks presented themselves as willing candidates for assimilation in society. The refusal of Blacks to violently respond to racism suggested that some were willing to act as Christians and forgive the injustices of Whites in Canada.

The church's role in promoting assimilation amongst Blacks was aided by the optimistic attitudes of Blacks. Many Blacks after settling in the 'Promised Land' were interested in creating a 'new Jerusalem' and the Black settlements with Black churches provided the ideal forum to achieve this utopia. The perseverance and dedication displayed in the churches located in these settlements are proof of a people desiring to begin a new life. Maybe some of their experiences were attempts to recreate a life in Africa which they heard from their parents and grandparents. They were in a new environment where the reminders of sugar and cotton were no longer present; where the master's house, once the main building, was substituted by the church and the whip by the Bible.

There was a genuine attempt by Blacks to be integrated into Canadian society. Most had no qualms about inter-ethnic relationships. For example, Jacob Dover, a 23 year old Black from Fergus, placed a newspaper advertisement seeking "an amiable young, white wife" who was of English, Irish or Scottish descent.[119] Blacks were willing to make sacrifices and live peacefully in a free land. During the 1830s there is ample evidence suggesting that Whites were not judging the Blacks based on the criteria of skin colour, an illustration is the admiration of Mary O'Brien of a Black in the locale, "...he is a man of great respectability and command amongst the men of his colour and interests us by his anxiety about his family."[120] Such accounts were not isolated incidents as another described a Black barber who was, "...married to a coloured woman and they are respectable, well-behaved people." Such accounts demonstrated the positive image of Blacks in Canada.[121] Within the church there was also a certain level of tolerance such as the Amherstburg Coloured Church which employed its only White minister, Rev. William Pott in 1871. The potential divisiveness of ethnicity did not materialise as Rev. Pott was able to faithfully serve the Amherstburg mission without encountering any prejudices at this Black Baptist Church.[122] This is an indicator of the open-mindedness of Blacks.

The attitude and mentality of Blacks in Canada complemented the efforts of the White church in promoting assimilation in society. The teachings of "practise what you preach" and "turn the other cheek" became an integral part in the lives of many Blacks as they hoped to increase their chances of assimilation. Wilfred Sheffield identified this Christ-like attitude prevailing among the Black Baptists, "Their charity to the sick and poverty-stricken newcomers was evidence of their religion in action as well as their courteous attitude to women and the lack of a revengeful spirit in all matters."[123] This view is supported by S.G. Howe's account, "... the religious instinct manifested itself in the form of pious work and the performance of duty, rather than in mere emotion and noisy demonstration."[124] Blacks would have hoped that by adopting this stance there would be a reduction of discrimination against the Black population. Redeeming qualities of Blacks served to reduce the negative perceptions held by Whites. Indeed, Blacks striving for and possessing prized qualities as honesty and obedience were able to manoeuvre themselves through a tense and volatile environment.

One aspect of the religious relationship that has been overlooked is the effect of the White church on the stability of the Black settlements. The daily life of the Blacks orbited around the church. Applicable to the work of the churches among Blacks is William Westfall's analysis of the Protestant culture in the nineteenth century especially the symbiotic relationship between church and state. He contended that the creation of faithful, law-abiding citizens was a goal of a Christian society and complemented the state's implementation of laws to promote discipline.[125] From the inception of Black settlements, be it rural or urban, the Protestant Church became an integral part in the life of Blacks. In many instances it seemed that the affiliation to a specific Protestant denomination and local church curbed the migratory tendencies of the Blacks who might have otherwise sought better economic and social conditions outside the settlement or township.[126] There is also the need to consider the effect kinship ties and prosperity had on the internal migration of Blacks. In the United States, kinship ties reduced migration of Blacks, "So long as a black family remained together upon one plantation, their love for one another operated as the strongest bond to prevent their departure."[127]

Chatham was seen as a place in which Blacks could make a decent living and thus there was not as much relocating of Blacks in this area.[128]

The location of settlements was another factor which accounted for reduced migration. For instance, fertile land in Chatham attracted farmers and its geographical isolation ensured protection against catchers of the enslaved.[129] The weekly attendance of families and their financial contributions to the well-being of a local church increased their attachment to the missions. The church can be credited for nurturing this linkage between Blacks and Christianity and aided the factors which contributed to the stability of the settlement.

Certain individuals openly supported efforts for successful assimilation. In the early history of the First Baptist Church in Toronto the initial services were attended by both races.[130] During this transitional era, staunch supporters of integration included both White and Black leaders such as Reverends Michael Willis, Hiram Wilson and Henry Bibb. Also belonging to this cadre were George Whipple, Secretary of the AMA, and Rev. Michael Willis, President of the Anti-Slavery Society of Canada. These proponents of integration ensured that racially mixed schools and churches would become a reality. King boasted that in the St. Andrews Church at Buxton, both ethnic groups worshipped without segregation and at the weekly prayer meetings there was an absence of racial division.[131] Such incidents would be exceptions rather than the norm in Canada. In King's letter to the *Ecclesiastical and Missionary Record*, he revealed that on the opening of the Sabbath school with its ten pupils, there was a mixture of Whites and Blacks.[132] Such noteworthy acts promoted assimilation and provided a fertile ground for racial tolerance.

One of the obstacles to assimilation was the phenomenon of interdenominational rivalry. Rev. J.P. Bardwell of the AMA, who served in London, recalled the division of the Black community among three Christian denominations. Nevertheless, it was to the advantage of Blacks that this friction did not develop into serious schisms. During the 1830s, there was an increasing intolerance towards Roman Catholicism in Upper Canada and this sentiment persisted throughout the nineteenth century. Among the Protestants a similar antagonism existed as was the case with the disapproval of Presbyterians in Lancaster to the establishment of the Church of England in the province. The petition of Rev. Alexander McNaughton included 251 members of the Presbyterian congregation of Lancaster.[133]

Some churches accepted the belief that all churches were one in the body of Christ, whilst others felt the need to criticise conflicting doctrines and practices. During the nineteenth century there is no tangible evidence indicating that Blacks were attracted in large numbers to Roman Catholicism, thus their membership in the various Protestant denominations gave them a reprieve from the prevailing anti-Catholic sentiment in Upper Canada. The absence of crippling divisions among Blacks in terms of class, education, race/ethnicity and colour reinforced Black unity. From the ashes of prejudice arose the unforeseen phoenix of unity among Blacks, "They declared openly that their God would deliver and protect them, and that He was not found in a particular denomination."[134]

Religious and secular education of Blacks seemed to succumb to the prevailing prejudices. It was only through the intervention of Sabbath and mission schools that Blacks and their children were afforded an unimpeded opportunity to assimilate into society. Unfortunately there were few White churches that adhered to the belief of racial equality. Thus only a limited number of Blacks were exposed to the sincerity of Whites. Segregated churches and burial plots proved to be one of the toughest challenges and to circumvent this ordeal, without severe repercussions demanded considerable toleration and accommodation. Malcolm Wallace suggested, "Although there was unlimited Canadian enthusiasm for providing a refuge for the colored man, he was as a rule, segregated in church, school and social relationships...."[135]

Some believed that Christianity positively influenced Blacks, "Thus the desire to imitate the higher civilization around them, seconded by the influence of the church, has brought the colored people rapidly up, and out of their loose and incontinent habits."[136] For many Blacks, religion served as a moral blueprint to mould their lives into worthy subjects. Among Blacks the absence of verbal outbursts, riots or protests suggested that the basis of their faith was not superficial. Religion did not merely diminish the possibility of social disorder but created a cadre of morally upright Black citizens; it not only ensured their assimilation into society and led to the eventual sharing of the mantle of church leadership.

Notes

[1] See Don McKinney, "Getting Along in Antebellum Georgian Slavery: Dimensions of the Moral Life Heard in the Voices of the Slaves Themselves" (PhD diss,. Vanderbilt University, 1992).

[2] See Clinton Stockwell, "A Better Class of People: Protestants in the Shaping of Early Chicago, 1833-1873" (PhD diss., University of Illinois at Chicago, 1992).

[3] Fourteenth Report of the American Missionary Association 1860, np.

[4] See John Grant, *A Profusion of Spires: Religion in Nineteenth Century Ontario* (Toronto: University of Toronto Press, 1988), 110. During this time the Methodists avoided the condemnation of slavery; Winks, *Blacks in Canada*, 355.

[5] Farrell, "History of the Negro Community in Chatham," 190. See also "Mission to the Free Coloured Population" Occasional Paper, 1. February 1854, 4. Conditions did not seem to change. An analysis of the Blacks in Halifax during the 1960s revealed that education, equal status contact in a non-competitive environment produces a low degree of racial hostility. Jennie Tarlo, "Racial antipathy in an Urban Environment" (MA thesis, Dalhousie University, 1968), 105.

[6] Wright, *African Americans in the Colonial Era*, 97.

[7] Johnson 87. "That prejudice against them among the whites (including the English) is engendered by the same circumstances, and manifested with the same intensity, as in the United States." Howe 102.

[8] Clairmont and Magill 112.

[9] Walker, *Black Identity*, 10.

[10] See Winks, *Blacks in Canada*, 142-143.

[11] Landon, "Anti-Slavery Society of Canada," 126.

[12] Hill, "Negroes Sociological Study," 339. Hill mentioned the fear among Canadian Blacks and Whites after the passage of the Fugitive Slave Act. Appendix C "Reaction of the Negro Community Towards Arrival of Fugitive Slaves during the 1850s," 368.

[13] Second Annual Report presented to the Anti-Slavery Society of Canada, March 23, 1853, 8.

[14] David Savage, *The Life and Labours of the Reverend William McClure* (Toronto, 1872), 202. William Caven, "The Rev. Michael Willis," *Knox College Monthly* 4 (1886): 100. Law 110.

[15] See Winks, *Blacks in Canada*, 338.

[16] "Negro societies in Canada." McCurdy Papers, AO. See also Wilbur H. Siebert, *The Underground Railroad from Slavery to Freedom* (New York: Russell and Russell, 1898), 230-231.

[17] Drew 236.

[18] Elgersman 149.

[19] *Ecclesiastical and Missionary Record*, May 1848.

[20] Walton 71.

[21] See Mary Garman, "'Altered Tone of Expression': The Anti-Slavery Rhetoric of Illinois Women, 1837-1847" (PhD diss., Northwestern University, 1989).

[22] See Karen Halbersleben, "'She Hath Done What She Could,': Women's Participation in the British Antislavery Movement, 1825-1870" (PhD diss., State University of New York, 1987).

[23] See John Quist, "Social and Moral Reform in the Old North and the Old South: Washtenaw County, Michigan and Tuscaloosa County, Alabama, 1820-1860" (PhD diss., University of Michigan, 1992).

[24] Clairmont and Magill 112.

[25] Tulloch 120.

[26] Select committee appointed 20 January 1840, Upper Canada, House of Assembly. *Journal* 13th Parliament, 5th Session (1839-1840) Appendix, 28.

[27] Constitution and Bylaws of the Wilberforce Lyceum Educating Society for Moral and Mental Improvement (Amherstburg, 1850)1, Baldwin Room. Metropolitan Library, Toronto.

[28] Roger 408.

[29] Law 113.

[30] Carlesimo 157.

[31] Howe 92.

[32] *Provincial Freeman*, March 24, 1854.

[33] Sixth Annual Report of the Buxton Mission, presented at the meeting of the Synod, 16 June 1856. *Ecclesiastical and Missionary Record*, October 1856.

[34] *Knox College Monthly* 11 (1889): 36.

[35] Shreve 72.

[36] Winks, *Blacks in Canada*, 210.

[37] An Act to Incorporate the Elgin Association for the Settlement and Moral Improvement of the Coloured Population of Canada, 10 August 1850.

[38] *Voice of the Fugitive*, January 15, 1851. Landon, "Negro migration to Canada," 35.

[39] *Douglass Monthly*, April 1859.

[40] *Douglass Monthly*, May 1859.

[41] *British Constitution*, December 9, 1864.

[42] Wilfred Sheffield, "Background and Development of Negro Baptists in Ontario" (MA thesis, McMaster University, 1952), 25.

[43] Carlesimo 161.

[44] Ibid., 182.

[45] *Provincial Freeman*, April 18, 1857.

[46] Alexander Murray, "Canada and the Anglo-American Anti-Slavery Movement: A Study In International Philanthropy" (PhD diss., University of Pennsylvania, 1960), 237.

[47] Elgersman 147.

[48] "Black Nova Scotian odyssey" 81.

[49] Grant 258.

[50] Ibid.

[51] Lamin Sanneh, *West African Christianity: The Religious Impact* (New York: Orbis, 1983), 68.

[52] Blassingame 133.

[53] See Ged Martin, "British Officials and Their Attitudes to the Negro Community in Canada 1833-1861," *Ontario History* 66 (1974): 79-88. See also Winks, "Negro School Segregation," 164-191; Allen P. Stouffer, "'A Restless Child of Change and Accident': The Black Image in Nineteenth Century Ontario," *Ontario History* 76 (1984): 128-150; James W. St. G. Walker, *Racial Discrimination in Canada: The Black Experience* (Ottawa: Canadian Historical Association Booklet, 1985).

[54] In the United States, even though Black and White preachers often ministered to their own race, there was no rigid separation of both races. David Bruce, *And they all sang Hallelujah: Plain-folk camp-meeting religion 1800-1845* (Knoxville, 1974), 74-75.

[55] Winks, "Negroes in the Maritimes," 464-465.

[56] *New York Age*, 12 March 1892 in Abbott Papers, Metropolitan Reference Library, Toronto.

[57] Colin Thomson, *Blacks in Deep Snow: Black Pioneers in Canada* (Don Mills: J.M Dent and Sons, 1979), 46-47.

[58] *Dumfries Reformer*, August 5, 1863.

[59] Walton 197.

[60] Steward 269.

[61] For evidence that discrimination played an important role in return migration see Simpson, "Negroes in Ontario," 17. King 437-439. Walton 165.

[62] Walton 234.

[63] Howe 102.

[64] John Zucchi, *Italians in Toronto-Development of a National Identity 1875-1895* (Montreal, McGill-Queen's University Press, 1988) 198. There is the belief that Blacks displayed an ambivalence towards Canada. Winks, *Blacks in Canada*, 144.

[65] Simpson, "Negroes in Ontario," 898.

[66] Minutes of the Eleventh Annual Conference of the BME Church, (Toronto, 1867), 4-5.

[67] "Neither slavery nor involuntary servitude, except as a punishment for a crime whereof the party shall have been duly convicted, shall exist within the United States, or any place subject to their jurisdiction." Section 1, Thirteenth Amendment, 1865. With the passage of the Fourteenth Amendment the slaves gained the right to vote and citizenship. Under this amendment, discriminatory legislation such as the Black Codes were attacked, "No state shall make or enforce any law which shall abridge the privileges or immunities of citizens of the United States; nor shall any State deprive any person of life, or property without due process of law." Section 1. Fourteenth Amendment, 1868. "The right of citizens of the United States to vote shall not be denied or abridged by the United States or by any State on the account of race, color, or previous condition of servitude." Section 1, Fifteenth Amendment, 1870. The First Reconstruction Act of 1867 divided the former Confederacy into five sections and required that the former states implement constitutions guaranteeing all Blacks the right to vote. Due to the refusal of Southern Whites to give Blacks the right to vote, a Second Reconstruction Act in 1868 was passed utilising the military in voting procedures.

[68] Catherine Brooks, "Negro Colonization Projects and Settlements in Canada until 1865" (MA thesis, Howard University, 1945), 76.

[69] Walton 233; Roger 405.

[70] Seventh Report of the American Missionary Association 1853. Fred Landon Papers, University of Western Ontario.

[71] See April 5, 1847. Hodgins Papers, AO

[72] *Chatham Journal*, December 5, 1858.

[73] Address by William McCrae. "A Public Meeting Being Held in Chatham on the 18th., pursuant to requisition, addressed to John Waddell, Esq. Sheriff, W.D to take into consideration the scheme proposed by the Elgin Association, for settling the Township of Raleigh with Negroes...." (Chatham, 1850) Baldwin Room,

Metropolitan Library, Toronto. There is the contention that Whites in Chatham were racist. Walton 23.

[74] *Elora Observer*, April 7, 1865. See also Jerome Teelucksingh, "Upper Canada's Black Presence," *Families* 41 (2002): 218.

[75] *Elora Observer*, April 29, 1864.

[76] See Robert Hall, "'Do Lord, Remember Me': Religion and Cultural Change Among Blacks in Florida, 1565-1906" (PhD diss., Florida State University, 1984).

[77] See James Black, "Contours of Faith: An Intellectual and Social Profile of the Georgia Baptist Association, 1820-1860" (MA thesis, California State University, Long Beach, 1996).

[78] Jennifer West, "'Before We Reach the Heavenly Fields': Religion and Society in Wilkes County, Georgia, 1783-1881" (PhD diss., Emory University, 1995).

[79] See Sensbach, "Separate Canaan."

[80] Wright, *African Americans in the Colonial Era*, 96.

[81] *Chatham Gleane*r, November 21, 1848.

[82] Other immigrant groups such as the French would have been a minority group and also faced obstacles as linguistic and cultural barriers in Upper Canada.

[83] See Chapter 6 in John Jackson, "Black Religion: A Living Gestalt" (PhD diss., Seattle University, 1988)

[84] Anniversary brochure of The First Baptist Church, Huron Street, Toronto (165 years old) 1826-1991. See also Spencer 55-60.

[85] Peter Paris, *The Moral, Political and religious Significance of the Black Churches in Nova Scotia* (Dartmouth: Black Cultural Centre for Nova Scotia),7.

[86] See Norman McRae, "Blacks in Detroit, 1736-1833: The Search for Freedom and Community and its Implications for Educators" (PhD diss., University of Michigan, 1982).

[87] Rabinowitz 201.

[88] James W. St. G. Walker, *The Black Loyalists: The Search for a Promised Land in Nova Scotia and Sierra Leone 1783-1870* (Halifax: Dalhousie University Press, 1976), 67-68.

[89] George Eaton Simpson, *Black Religions in the New World* (New York: Columbia University Press, 1978), 248.

[90] Elgersman 148.

[91] Walker, *Black Identity*, 9.

[92] Thomson 47. Winks, *Blacks in Canada*, 338.

[93] Howe 102. In a letter to the editor of the Globe there is one incident in Toronto of a coloured man being denied a seat in a pew in a Methodist Church. *Globe*, September 24, 1853. See *Provincial Freeman*, March 25, 1854.

[94] "Mission to the Free Coloured Population," Occasional Paper no. 2 December 1854, 10.

[95] See *Kitchener-Waterloo Record*, July 17, 1997; *Citizen*, April 3, 1991; *Kitchener-Waterloo Record*, July 20, 1979; *Brantford Exposition*, June 18, 1943; Peel Township Tombstone Transcriptions located at Wellington County Archives, Fergus.

[96] *The Gazette*, January 25, 1997.

---

[97] *Sun Times*, April 20, 1998. Location of this cemetery is at the intersection of Durham Road and County Road 14 in Artemesia Township.

[98] Winks, *Blacks in Canada*, 338.

[99] "History of Negro Migration to Canada" Notebook, Abbott Papers, Metropolitan Library, Toronto.

[100] Letter from J.G. Birney to Lewis Tappan, Buffalo, July 14, 1837 in *Letters of J.G Birney* vol. 1, 395-396. Fred Landon Papers, University of Western Ontario.

[101] Rabinowitz 201.

[102] Rabinowitz 107.

[103] Winks, *Blacks in Canada*, 338.

[104] Rabinowitz 203.

[105] Winks, *Blacks in Canada*, 341-342.

[106] Paris 3.

[107] Journal of Benjamin Slight May 12, 1835, 106. UCA.

[108] See Abbott Papers, Baldwin Room, Metropolitan Library, Toronto.

[109] Hill, "Negroes in Toronto," 78.

[110] J.C. Hamilton, "The African in Canada," *Knox College Monthly* 11 (November 1889): 31. Also Drew 371; *Provincial Freeman*, November 24, 1855.

[111] Nitkin 120.

[112] "The African Methodist Episcopal Church in Edgar, Ontario," *Akili* 2 (1994): 7.

[113] Alexander and Glaze 64.

[114] Landon, "The Wilberforce Refugee Colony" 31; see William H and Jane Pease, "Opposition to the Founding of the Elgin Settlement," *Canadian Historical Review* 38 (1957): 202-218.

[115] *Ecclesiastical and Missionary Record*, January 1849.

[116] Paris 26.

[117] Journal of Benjamin Slight, November 14, 1834. vol. 1, 56-57, 71. UCA. He also mentioned a Society which comprised 10 Whites, 26 Indians and 6 Black persons.

[118] Report of the Committee on Emigration of the Amherstburg Convention - Presented at the First Baptist Church, Amherstburg, Canada West June 17, 1853. From Minutes and Proceedings of the General Convention for the Improvement Of the Coloured Inhabitants of Canada held in Amherstburg, Canada West, 16 and 17 June 1853, (Windsor, 1853) 12-14.

[119] *British Constitution and Fergus Freeholder*, January 9, 1858.

[120] Journal 69. May 7, 1832, 2. Mary O'Brien Papers, AO.

[121] W.L. MacKenzie, *Sketches of Canada and the United States* (London, 1833), 19.

[122] "Amherstburg Coloured Church Shows Progress In Past Century" Speech by Norma Wilson at centenary of church, 3. McCurdy Papers, AO.

[123] Sheffield 36.

[124] Howe 92. He also mentions their "forgiving tempers and their affectionate dispositions." 97. See also Ruth D. Wilson, "Negro-White Relations in Western Ontario," *Negro History Bulletin* 18 (1955): 105-106.

[125] Westfall 22.

[126] The majority of names appear on the rolls during these years indicating reduced migration during these four years. Assessment Rolls for the Township of Colchester 1845-1849.

[127] Marion MacDougal, *Fugitive Slaves* (1619-1865) (rep. New York: Bergman Publishers, 1967), 55.

[128] Walton 127.

[129] Walton 25, 26.

[130] J.R. Robertson, *Landmarks of Toronto: A Collection of Historical Sketches of the Old Town of York from 1792-1837 and of Toronto from 1837-1904* (Toronto: np, 1904), 471-472.

[131] *Autobiography of King*, 296-297.

[132] *Ecclesiastical and Missionary Record*, February 1850.

[133] In 1831 petitions were presented objecting to the growth of Catholicism and other non-British religions in the province. Upper Canada. House of Assembly *Journal* 11th Parliament, 1st session (1831) Appendix, 179. Upper Canada House of Assembly *Journal*. 13th Parliament, 1st Session (1836-1837) 408-410. See also Westfall 22. Grant 204, 206.

[134] Lewis 4.

[135] Malcolm Wallace, "Pioneers of the Scotch Settlement on the Shore of Lake St. Clair," *Ontario History* (1949): 196.

[136] Howe 32.

CONCLUSION

The presence of most Blacks in Canada was due to their escape from the drudgery of plantation life and oppressive discrimination practices in the United States. Indeed, slavery in the United States contained elements of its destruction. Harsh and brutal treatment of enslaved persons aroused compassion and sympathy among Whites in North America and Britain.

The abolition of slavery in the United States was not due solely to Abraham Lincoln's Emancipation Proclamation of 1863 and the Civil War. Instead, Canada and the Underground Railroad proved to be the weak links in the long and heavy chain of slavery. Regular utilisation of the Underground Railroad undermined the stranglehold of slavery on the economy of the United States. The escape was a psychological victory over the oppressive system which preceded the physical liberation of the Blacks. If the Underground Railroad had not existed and Canada decided to close its borders to the Black refugees, then there is the possibility that slavery in the United States would have continued into the twentieth century.

The harrowing experiences during slavery had a powerful influence on the religious attitudes of Blacks in Canada. And this was often instrumental in invoking a desire to be empowered with educational and leadership skills. For most Blacks, the denial of religious and educational instruction in the United States was pivotal in understanding their attraction to religion in Canada. Blacks were acutely aware that religion was the key that opened the doors to limited social and occupational mobility. Education and Black leadership had become a two-edged sword cutting away at ignorance, inferiority and illiteracy. The relatively high numbers of Blacks in congregations was proof that Christianity in Canada was neither confined to serving a particular class nor ethnic group. Most of these Blacks were either illiterate or inexperienced leaders, yet the White Protestant Church in Canada embraced them and provided a relatively congenial atmosphere in which the Blacks were sometimes given an opportunity to procure an education and become leaders ministering to their people.

Any study of the Protestant Church's mission among Blacks in Canada would reveal the interconnectedness among religion, education, leadership, assimilation and management skills. It would be difficult to conceptualise Black leaders, having been protected and taught by Whites, as not being able to achieve a limited form of assimilation in Canada. Leadership and independence of Black churches could not prevail without education, as Black leaders would be incapable of reading and preaching from the Bible.

The compatibility and inseparability of religion and education proved to be the basis for the empowerment of Blacks. In Canada, the Protestant Church's provision of education made Blacks more appreciative of the work in their settlements. Undoubtedly, the separate schools restricted the rate of assimilation of Blacks in Canadian society, however, the church performed a multi-functional role as a stabilising force, a protector and friend in the life of the Blacks. Undoubtedly, the service, dedication and commitment to the education and protection of Blacks clearly demonstrated the paternalistic nature of some Whites.

A significant theme in the development of Black Christianity in Canada is the gradual emergence and grooming of Black leaders. Indeed, they had partially internalised the mores of the White parent churches and their leaders. The development of Black leadership and the ensuing successful transition of religious authority from Whites to Blacks transformed the public image of Blacks. The standards, styles and strategies which Blacks adopted from their White counterparts were proof of acculturation. The contributions of itinerant Black preachers from the United States ensured the survival of mission stations during a critical phase of growth.

The arduous task of judging the Protestant Church's mission among Blacks as a promoter of integration or segregation is one that would generate considerable debate among scholars. Most of the Whites in Protestant churches were guilty of discrimination especially with the existence of segregated pews and burial plots. But these proved to be a blessing in disguise as it coaxed the managerial skills and leadership qualities from the Blacks which led to the rapid rise of independent Black churches. Indeed, the apparent negativism served as a catalyst to hasten the emergence of a unique Black church in Canada. Paradoxically, the all-Black settlements which initially protected Blacks from racially-provoked attacks, considerably reduced interracial interaction and tended to promote isolation.

In Canada, the Protestant Church was unable to free itself from the influence of a predominantly anti-Black sentiment. Sabbath schools and some congregations freely allowed intermingling amongst the races/ethnicities and this aspect of assimilation counteracted the Church's negative image. Undoubtedly, Whites in leadership positions such as Revs.

Slight, King, Wilson and Willis were fierce advocates of anti-slavery, integrationists and stalwart supporters of education and the grooming of future Black leaders. Also, the philanthropy of magnanimous Whites and those involved in charitable groups cannot be easily ignored and greatly outweighed the stigma of racism and intolerance among some of the Whites.

Among the many immigrant groups who entered Canada during the nineteenth century, the Blacks from the United States were unique as no other group of settlers had escaped from the trauma and horrors of slavery. Stereotypes of social deviance, uncleanliness and illiteracy coupled with anti-Semitism, xenophobia and isolationism were part of the unfriendly immigration backlash endured by the waves of Asians, Russians, Italians, Jews and Austro-Hungarian immigrants in the late nineteenth and early twentieth centuries.

As a sign of gratitude for the deliverance from slavery, the enthusiastic response of Blacks to life in Canada was unmatched by any other minority group in the nineteenth century. The role of religion as a dynamic force in the lives of Blacks was evident in their indifference to acts of discrimination and prejudice. If compared to other immigrants as the Irish Catholics in the nineteenth century, the Blacks would consider themselves fortunate to be under the protective umbrella of sympathetic churches which shielded them from the brunt of anti-Black sentiment existing in Canadian society. It was the daily survival in such a relatively hostile scenario which constantly tested their faith.

The missionary arm of the church encapsulated proselytising in its educational mission and social outreach. For many Blacks, life in Canada was not restricted to religion. Each day was a learning experience bearing new challenges. Religion seemed to provide some of the solutions to resolving problems and diffusing tensions. Black leaders and their congregations had a resilient, yet passive and tolerant attitude which facilitated their emotional growth and social interaction. Blacks were fortunate that their victories would be intact and pervasive whilst their religious experiences would be meaningful and productive.

Some Blacks would have been unaware of the subtle but critical effect that religion had on their lives. Religion inevitably contributed to the cohesion of the Black settlements and benefits were accrued beyond the realm of the schools and churches. The advantages of Protestantism in Canada, when compared to Roman Catholicism, was its superior record of faithfully serving the Blacks. The flexibility of the Protestant church is best illustrated in its astounding ability to act as protector, educator, friend and guide of the Blacks whilst socializing, spiritually nurturing and guiding Blacks.

In Canada, the church's multifaceted role in education, development of leadership and assimilation led to a secure and meaningful future for Blacks. Though many Blacks were deprived, alienated, humiliated and scorned during slavery, in Canada they were able to bravely overcome the trauma and psychological damage and remarkably adapt to their new host society. In understanding the religious axis of Blacks, there is the impression of an inseparable relationship which has been occasionally tested and progressively strengthened.

In Canada, the umbilical cord between Blacks and Christianity produced lasting benefits in the realms of secular and religious education. The crux of religion and Blacks is an account which is inextricably bound to their forced migration to Canada. For Canada's role in harbouring these Blacks, the country deserved international recognition and respect for its humanitarian efforts during the anti-slavery struggle.

Appendix A

Muster Book of Free-Black Settlement of Birchtown, Port Rosaway. Muster 3 and 4 July 1784

Heads of Families

Edward Cox
John Thomas (dead)

Charles Bailey
Jupiter Carminian
Daniel Barclay
John Green
William O'Neal (sic)

Jacob Barrent
Thomas Evans
Dublin Gordon
John Banburry
Thomas Kane

Abigail Newton
Hannah Miller
Peggy Campbell
John Williams
Abraham Crie
John Thomas
James Le Gray

William Ash
Richard Ball
Robert Jackson
Betty Tucker

Women and children

Elizabeth Thomas
Christina Thomas
Bristol Peterson
John Peterson

Hannah Jackson
Judith Jackson

Lydia O'Neil
Jenny O'Neil

Abigail Moore
Peggy Moore
Jenny Roberts
Judith Evans
Sarah Evans
Thomas Evans
Abigail Spur
Frank Spur
Lucy Banbury
Nancy Moody
Sarah Miles
Venus Le Gray
William Le Gray
Mary Ash
Esther Ash

Source: Letter from Stephen Blucke to Major Skinner. Birchtown, December 15, 1790.

APPENDIX B

Return for Negroes and their families mustered in Annapolis County 28 May and 30 June 1784

Refugee Blacks who settled at Digby

John Holland
John Prince
John Williams
John Sampson
Henry White
Willey White
John Shepherd
Jos. Leonard
Ja. Liverpool
James Austin
Adam Biggs
Carey Mead
Jos. Mason
Isaac Mason
Laury Mason
Prince Mason
Sam Farmer
Bristol Godfrey
Henry Mitchel
Thomas Bing
John Godfrey
Daphne Shells
Niles Jordan
John Jordan
John Babus
Benjamin Bush
John Curtis

Black Pioneers arriving in the ship Joseph and intending to settle at Digby

Big John
James Bowls
Serj. Peters
Sue Mott
Violet Moore

Black Pioneers living at Annapolis

Grace Mason
Robert Harris
Elizabeth Williams
Nancy Jackson
Serjeant Steele
William Catchpole
John Pratt
James Stroke
Liberty Stroke
Levi Stroke
Jobo Stroke
Jacob Wilkinson
Fanny Brown

Refugee Blacks residing in Annapolis and Granville

Tho. Ragg
Peter Human
Dempsey Slater
Ishmael Slater
Dick Slater
Aberdeen Slater
Dick Vanwart
Mansfield Vanwart

Source: Ward Chipman Papers, Muster Master General's Office- Loyalist Musters 1776-1785.

APPENDIX C

Tables indicating the Black population during 1860-1861

The census of 1860-1861 indicates that the total coloured population in Upper Canada was 11,223.

(Source: Census of the Canadas 1860-1861. Vol. 1 Quebec: S.B Foote, 1863. Appendix to Census of Canada no. 2 Census of Origin). See also Jerome Teelucksingh, "Coloured Families in Upper Canada 1860-1861," *Families* 41.1 (2002) 33-34.

Table 1 County of Essex

Town of Amherstburgh	318
Anderdon	551
Colchester	728
Gosfield	87
Maidstone	375
Malden	276
Sandwich, East	455
Sandwich, West	50
Town of Windsor	541

Table 2 County of Kent

Town of Chatham	1,770
Chatham and Gore	736
Dover	211
Harwich	508

Table 3 County of Wellington

Amaranth	4
Elora	9
Eramosa	16
Erin	17
Garafraxa	7
Town of Guelph	38
Luther	14

APPENDIX D

Table illustrating the number of Blacks in Upper Canadian settlements

Settlement	Year and number of Blacks		
	1852	1856	1860
Amherstburg	400-500	800	
Hamilton	800	274	600
Galt	-----	40	
Colchester Village	1200	450 (Colchester)	
St. Catharines	800	200-250	
(and Niagara)	1500 (combined)		
London	350	500	
Gosfield	78		
Toronto	800	1,000	1,600
Chatham	800	2,000	
Buxton	800	800	
Dresden, Dawn Settlement	500	70	
Windsor	50	2,500	
Sandwich	300	100	2,000

Source: Compiled from the First Annual Report of the Anti-Slavery Society, 1852, 16-17 and Drew *North Side View of Slavery*, 17, 94, 118, 136, 147, 234, 291, 308, 321, 341, 348, 367. Spencer, "Black Education," 53-54. Landon, "Social Conditions Among the Negroes," 146.

APPENDIX E

Table illustrating the British Methodist Episcopal Church's mission stations among Blacks and the need for permanent Black leaders to minister to the congregations. Compiled by Rev. E. Crosbey, William Jones and Samuel Brown. Minutes of the AME Conference July 13, 1852. p.5

See also Jerome Teelucksingh, "Family Connections in British Methodist Schools and Churches during 1852," *Families* 43.1 (2004) 35-36.

Saint Catharines Station	S. H. Brown
St. Catharines	170
Drummondville	20
Fall	20
North Grand River	30
Dunnville	11
Total	251

London Station	H.E. Stevens
London	44
Norwich	12
Simcoe	114
Total	170

Chatham Station	R. Warren
Chatham	130
Dawn	35
Elgin	30
Total	195

Hamilton Station	Henry Dawson
Hamilton	47
Queens Bush	49
Total	96

Toronto Station	L. Taylor
Toronto	83
Total	83

APPENDIX F

Table indicating the location and dates of the British Methodist Episcopal Church's Annual Conferences.

15th Peel	July 13 1853
16th Chatham	July 21-30, 1855.
18th Chatham	September 29, 1856
2nd St. Catherines	September 5, 1857.
3rd Toronto	September 1, 1858.
4th Chatham	August, 1859.
5th Windsor	April, 1861.
6th London	June 17, 1862
7th Hamilton	June 23, 1863
8th Windsor	August 27 1864
9th n.p	June 3, 1865
10th Hamilton	May 26, 1866
11th Toronto	May 25, 1867.
12th Chatham	June 13, 1868
13th Windsor	May 29-June7, 1869
14th London	June 11, 1870

APPENDIX G

Table indicating Sessions of Annual and General Conferences of the British Methodist Episcopal Church. See Jerome Teelucksingh, "Family Searches in British Methodist Episcopal Church Literature," *Families* 43 (2004) 34.

Time	Place	Presiding Officer	Gen. Secretary
Aug. 2, 1856	Chatham Bishop	W. Nazrey	Jos. Brooks
May 10, 1857	London	Bishop W. Nazrey	J. Johnson
May 12, 1858	Brantford	Rev. R.R. Disney	Bell Beveney
Aug.20, 1859	Chatham	Bishop Nazrey	Bell Beveney
Aug.24, 1860	St.Catherines	Bishop W. Nazrey	Bell Beveney
Sept.3, 1860	Toronto	Bishop W. Nazrey	Bell Beveney
Aug. 20, 1861	Toronto	Bishop W. Nazrey	Wm. H. Jones
June 17, 1862	London	Bishop W. Nazrey	Wm. H. Jones
June 23, 1863	Hamilton	Bishop W. Nazrey	T.W. Stringer
Aug. 27, 1864	Windsor	Bishop W. Nazrey	R.R. Disney
June 3, 1865	St. Catherines	Bishop W. Nazrey	R.R. Disney
June 3, 1866	Hamilton	Bishop W. Nazrey	R.R. Disney
May 25, 1867	Toronto	Bishop W. Nazrey	J.O Banyon
May 13, 1868	Chatham	Bishop W. Nazrey	J.O Banyon
July 31, 1868	Liverpool, N.S	Bishop W. Nazrey	J.O Banyon
May 29, 1869	Windsor	Bishop W. Nazrey	J.O Banyon
May 29, 1870	Windsor	Bishop W. Nazrey	R.R. Disney

APPENDIX H

Advertisements from Upper Canada

FUGITIVE SLAVES

IN

CANADA.

A PUBLIC MEETING WILL BE HELD IN

THE FREE CHURCH,

ON MONDAY EVENING,

AT SEVEN O'CLOCK.

THE REV. WILLIAM KING

AND MR. W. H. DAY,

AN EDUCATED GENTLEMAN OF COLOUR,

will address the Meeting on the Social and Moral
improvement of the Coloured Population in Canada.

☞ *A COLLECTION will be taken up in aid of
the above object.*

MUSSELBURGH, 18th November 1859.

J WALKER, Printer, Musselburgh.

860

FUGITIVE SLAVES
IN CANADA.

THE ELGIN SETTLEMENT.

THERE WILL BE A PUBLIC MEETING IN

FREE SOUTH LEITH CHURCH,

ON

THURSDAY EVENING NEXT, AT 7 O'CLOCK,

TO HEAR STATEMENTS FROM

THE REV. WILLIAM KING,

formerly a Slave Owner in Louisiana, United States, and

WILLIAM H. DAY, ESQ. M.A.,

A Deputation from Canada, whither the Thirty Thousand have fled, escaping
from American Slavery.

The Rev. WILLIAM KING liberated his own Slaves, and in this respect
is mentioned in Mrs Harriet Beecher Stowe's work, "Dred," as "Clayton."

As this is a work of general benevolence—simply to give the Bible to
those in Canada who have heretofore been deprived of it—it is hoped that
there will be a large attendance at the Meeting.

   November 1859.   Barrell & Byers, Printers, Leith.

863

FUGITIVE SLAVES
IN
CANADA.

BUXTON MISSION.

A PUBLIC MEETING
WILL BE HELD IN THE

FREE CHURCH
GEORGE STREET, DUMFRIES,

On MONDAY Evening, September 3d,
At Eight o'Clock, when the

REV. WILLIAM KING
Formerly a Slave-owner in Louisiana, United States,

Will Address the Meeting on the subject of

Slavery in the United States, and the Social and Moral Improvement of the Fugitive Slaves in Canada.

At the close of the address a Collection will be taken up in aid of the Mission and Schools at Buxton, Canada West.

Dumfries, August 29, 1860.

Dumfries—Printed at the Standard Office, by Walter Easton.

864

FUGITIVE SLAVES
IN CANADA.

There will be

A PUBLIC MEETING
ON
MONDAY Evening, 12th Dec,
At Eight o'Clock,

IN ST. THOMAS' CHURCH,
West Blackhall Street,
In behalf of Fugitive Slaves in Canada.

ADDRESSES will be then Delivered by

REV. WILLIAM KING,
formerly a Slave-owner in Louisiana, U.S., and

WM. HOWARD DAY, ESQ., M.A.,

A Deputation from the Elgin Settlement in Canada.

Rev. WM. KING is "The Clayton" of Mrs Harriet Beecher Stowe's work "Dred," having liberated his own Slaves, and taken them to British soil.

The Settlement was Established to give Homes to the Adults, and a Christian Education to the Children.

A COLLECTION WILL BE TAKEN AT THE CLOSE.

A CITY OF REFUGE
IN CANADA,
FOR AMERICAN SLAVES.

A PUBLIC MEETING
Will be held THIS EVENING (D.V.), at Seven o'Clock, in the TONTINE,

To receive a Deputation—the Rev. WM. KING, and Mr. WM. DAY, a gentleman of Colour—who will give information regarding the Slave Popula tion of America, and the Elgin Settlement in Canada—a city of refuge for the Negro Race.

You are earnestly requested to attend.

Armagh, Saturday, 8th Oct , 1859.   PRINTED AT THE ARMAGH GUARDIAN OFFICE

REFERENCES

Manuscripts

Ontario Provincial Archives. Toronto
    Alvin McCurdy Papers
    John Strachan Papers
    Niagara Historical Society Collection
    Mary O'Brien Journal
McMaster Divinity College. McMaster University, Hamilton.
    Amherstburg Baptist Association Minutes 1841-1861
    Covenant of the First Baptist Church, Sandwich.
Metropolitan Library, Toronto
    Abbott Papers
    First Baptist Church, Brantford. Minutes 1833-76.
    Constitution and Bylaws of the Wilberforce Lyceum Educating Society
Public Archives of Canada, Ottawa,
    Papers of Mary Ann Shadd Cary.
Public Archives of Nova Scotia
Presbyterian Church Archives, Toronto.
    Poster of Mathews Academy
    Autobiography of Rev. William King 1892.
    Minutes of the Presbyterian Church of Canada
United Church Archives
    Journal of Benjamin Slight vols. 1 and 2
Proceedings of the Thirteenth Session of the Annual Conference of the British Methodist Episcopal Church
University of Western Ontario Archives,
    Canadian Black Studies Project
    Letterbook of the Reverend Marmaduke Martin Dillon 1854-1856.
    Fred Landon Papers

Printed Minutes, Letters, Directories and Documents

Canada. Bureau of Dominion Statistics *Census of Canada* 1851,1861
Canada *Journals of the Legislative Assembly* 1831-1849

Canadian Anti-Slavery Baptist Association Constitution, bylaws, minutes for 1854

William McCrae A Public Meeting being held in Chatham to take into consideration the scheme proposed by the Elgin Association, for settling the Township of Raleigh with Negroes. Chronicle Office, Chatham: G.Gould,1850.

Minutes and Proceedings of the General Convention for the Improvement of the Coloured Inhabitants of Canada. Held by Adjournments in Amherstburg, Canada West. June 16 and 17 1853, Windsor: Canada West, 1853.

Dissertations

Aamodt, Terrie. "Righteous Armies, Holy Cause Apocalyptic Imager and the Civil War." PhD diss., Boston University, 1987.

Bascio, Patrick. "Black Theology: Its Critique of Classical or Scholastic Theology." PhD diss., Fordham University, 1987.

Bell, Earnest. "History of the Black Church in Detroit as a Study in American Public Address." PhD diss., Wayne State University, 1987.

Black, James. "Contours of Faith: An Intellectual and Social Profile of the Georgia Baptist Association, 1820-1860." MA thesis, California State University, Long Beach, 1996.

Blight, David. "Keeping the Faith in Jubilee: Frederick Douglass and the Meaning of the Civil War." PhD diss., University of Wisconsin-Madison, 1985.

Brooks, Catherine. "Negro Colonization Projects and Settlements in Canada until 1865." MA thesis, Howard University, 1945.

Burnet, Jean. "Ethnic Groups in Upper Canada." MA thesis, University of Toronto, 1943.

Carlesimo, Peter. "The Refugee Home Society: Its Origin, Operation and Results 1851-1876." MA thesis, University of Western Ontario, 1973.

Coleman, Willie. "A Study of African American Slave Narratives as a Source for a Contemporary, Constructive Black Theology." PhD diss., Graduate Theological Union, 1993.

Creed, John. "John Leland, American Prophet of Religious Individualism." PhD diss., Southwestern Baptist Theological Seminary, 1986.

Crowther, Edward. "Southern Protestants, Slavery and Secession: A Study in Religious Ideology, 1830-1861." PhD diss., Auburn University, 1986.

Denton, Virginia. "Booker T. Washington and the Adult Education Movement, 1856-1915." PhD diss., University of Southern Mississippi, 1988.

Devore, Donald. "Race Relations and Community Development: The Education of Blacks in New Orleans, 1862-1960." PhD diss., Louisiana State University and Agricultural and Mechanical College, 1989.

Elam, Richard. "Behold the Fields: Texas Baptists and the Problem of Slavery." PhD diss., University of North Texas, 1993.

Farrell, John. "The History of the Negro Community in Chatham, Ontario 1787-1865." PhD diss., University of Ottawa, 1955.

Garman, Mary. "'Altered Tone of Expression': The Anti-Slavery Rhetoric of Illinois Women, 1837-1847." PhD diss., Northwestern University, 1989.

Hall, Robert. "'Do Lord, Remember Me': Religion and Cultural Change Among Blacks in Florida, 1565-1906." PhD diss., Florida State University, 1984.

Halbersleben, Karen. "'She Hath Done What She Could,': Women's Participation in the British Antislavery Movement, 1825-1870." PhD diss., State University of New York, 1987.

Hildebrand, Reginald. "Methodism and the Meaning of Freedom: Missions to Southern Blacks during the era of Emancipation and Reconstruction." PhD diss., Princeton University, 1991.

Hill, Daniel. "Negroes in Toronto: A Sociological Study of a Minority Group." PhD diss., University of Toronto, 1960.

Hoogerwerf, Steven. "Forming the Character of Christian Discipleship: Singing the Lord's Song in a Strange Land." PhD diss., Duke University, 1991.

Hyman, Mark. "Afrocentric Leanings of Black Church-Owned Newspapers from mid-nineteenth Century to WW1." PhD diss, Temple University, 1992.

Jackson, John. "Black Religion: A Living Gestalt." PhD diss., Seattle University, 1988.

Jensen, Carole. "History of the Negro Community in Essex County 1850-1860." MA thesis, University of Windsor, 1966.

Johnson, Janice. "Leland University in New Orleans, 1870-1915." PhD diss., University of New Orleans, 1996.

Johnson, Lulu. "The Negro in Canada, Slave and Free." MA thesis, University of Iowa, 1930.

Kelly, Wayne. "Black Troops to Keep an Intelligent People in Awe!: The Coloured Companies of the Upper Canada Militia, 1837-1850." MA thesis, York University, 1996.

Landon, Fred. "The Relation of Canada to the Anti-Slavery and Abolition Movements in the United States." MA thesis, University of Western Ontario, 1919.

Lewis, James K. "The Religious Life of the Fugitive Slaves and the Rise of the Coloured Baptist Churches 1820-1865 in what is now known as Ontario." MA thesis, McMaster University, 1965.

Massey, Karen. "Ritual Improvisation: A Challenge to Christian Education from the Nineteenth Century African-American Slave Community." PhD diss., Southern Baptist Theological Seminary, 1991.

McKinney, Don. "Getting Along in Antebellum Georgian Slavery: Dimensions of the Moral Life Heard in the Voices of the Slaves Themselves." PhD diss,. Vanderbilt University, 1992.

McRae, Norman. "Blacks in Detroit, 1736-1833: The Search for Freedom and Community and its Implications for Educators." PhD diss., University of Michigan, 1982.

Murray, Alexander. "Canada and the Anglo-American Anti-Slavery Movement : A Study in International Philanthropy." PhD diss., University of Pennsylvania, 1960.

Neeley, Bobby. "Contemporary Afro-American Voodooism: The retention and Adaptation of the Ancient African-Egyptian Mystery System." PhD diss., University of California, Berkeley, 1988.

Nitkin, David. "Negro Colonization as a Response to Racism: A Historical Geography of the Southwestern Ontario Experience, 1830-1860." MA thesis, York University, 1973.

Owen, Christopher. "Sanctity, Slavery and Segregation: Methodists and Society in Nineteenth Century Georgia." PhD diss., Emory University, 1991.

Pemberton, I.C. "The Anti-Slavery Society of Canada." MA thesis, University of Toronto, 1967.

Quist, John. "Social and Moral Reform in the Old North and the Old South: Washtenaw County, Michigan and Tuscaloosa County, Alabama, 1820-1860." PhD diss., University of Michigan, 1992.

Ramey, Susan. "Salvation Black or White: Presbyterian Rationale and Protestant support for the Religious Instruction of Slaves in South Carolina." PhD diss., University of Nevada, 1994.

Roger, Sharon. "Slaves no More : A Study of the Buxton Settlement, Upper Canada 1849-1861." PhD diss., State University of New York at Buffalo, 1995.

Rogers, Bruce. "The Prophetic tradition in Nineteenth Century America: William Lloyd Garrison and Frederick Douglass." PhD diss., Drew University, 1992.

Sanders, Cheryl. "Slavery and Conversion: An Analysis of Ex-slave Testimony." PhD diss., Harvard University, 1985.

Sensbach, Jon. "A Separate Canaan: The Making of an Afro-Moravian World in North Carolina, 1763-1856." PhD diss., Duke University, 1991.

Sheffield, Wilfred. "Background and Development of Negro Baptists in Ontario." B.D thesis, McMaster University, 1952.

Silverman, Jason. "Unwelcome Guests : American Fugitive Slaves in Canada 1830-1860." PhD diss., University of Kentucky, 1981

Simpson, Donald. "Negroes in Ontario from Early Times to 1870." PhD diss., University of Western Ontario, 1971.

Snay, Mitchell. "Gospel of Disunion: Religion and the Rise of Southern Separatism, 1830-1861." PhD diss., Brandeis University, 1984.

Sparks, Randy. "A Mingled Yarn: Race and Religion in Mississippi, 1800-1876." PhD diss., Rice University, 1988.

Spencer, H.H. "To Nestle in the Mane of the British Lion: A History of Black Education, 1820-1870." PhD diss., Northwestern University, 1970.

Stennette, Janice. "Teaching for the Freedmen's Bureau: Lynchburg, Virginia, 1865-1871." PhD diss., University of Virginia, 1996.

Stockwell, Clinton. ""A Better Class of People: Protestants in the Shaping of Early Chicago, 1833-1873." PhD diss., University of Illinois at Chicago, 1992.

Tarlo, Jennie. "Racial Antipathy in an Urban Environment." MA thesis, Dalhousie University, 1968.

Walton, Jonathan. "Blacks in Buxton and Chatham 1830-1890: Did the 49th Parallel Make a Difference?" PhD diss., Princeton University, 1979.

Washington, James. "The Origins and Emergence of Black Baptist Separatism 1863-1897." PhD diss., Yale University, 1979.

Washington, Preston. "The Black Religious Imagination: A Theological and a Pedagogical Interpretation of the Afro-American Sermon in the Twentieth Century." PhD diss., Columbia University Teachers College, 1991.

White, Daryl. "Denominationalism, Politics and Social Class: An Anthropological Analysis of Southern Protestantism." PhD diss., University of Connecticut, 1985.

Williamson, Douglas. "The Ecclesiastical Career of Willbur Fisk: Methodist Educator, Theologian Reformer, Controversialist." PhD diss., Boston University, 1988.

Wright, Jeremiah A. "The Treatment of Biblical Passages in Negro Spirituals." MA thesis, Howard University, 1969.

Yeates, Marian. "Domesticating Slavery: Patterns of Cultural Rationalization in the Antebellum South, 1820-1860." PhD diss., Indiana University, 1996.

Ysursa, John. "'A Leap of Faith': Religion and the Coming of the American Civil War." PhD diss., University of California, 1996.

Young, Amy. "Risk and Material Conditions of American-American Saves at Locust Grove: An Archaeological Perspective." PhD diss., University of Tennessee, 1995.

Reports of Societies

American and Foreign Anti-Slavery Society *Annual Reports*.

Anti-Slavery Society of Canada *Annual Reports* 1852, 1853.

Colonial and Continental Church Society, Mission to Fugitive Slaves in Canada. *Annual Reports*. London. 1860-1864.

Eight Annual Report of the Directors of the Elgin Association

Minutes of the Annual Conferences of the British Methodist Episcopal Church.

Report of the Canadian Wesleyan Methodist New Connexion. Missionary Society in England Toronto: Watchman Office, 1852.

Reports of the American Missionary Association 1851, 1860, 1861.

Ryerson, Egerton, Annual Report of the Normal, Model and Common Schools in Upper Canada for the year 1852, *Sessional Papers of the Provincial Parliament of Canada*. Session 1853. Quebec: John Lovell, 1853.

The Majority and Minority Reports of the Committee on Slavery at the General Conference of the Methodist Episcopal Church. Buffalo: Sanford, Warren and Harroun, 1860.

Websites

http://www.duke.edu/~mahealey/black_canada.htm
http://www.blackhistoricalmuseum.com/undergroundrr.htm
http://www.niica.on.ca/csonan/BlackEvents.aspx
http://www.nowtoronto.com/issues/2001-07-12/news_spread.html

Pamphlets

Amherstburg Association. *Pathfinders of Liberty and Truth: A History of the Amherstburg Regular Missionary Baptist Association. Its Auxiliaries and Churches,* Amherstburg Association Historical Committee, 1940

Anniversary brochures of churches belonging to the Amherstburg Baptist Association.

Brown, Paola. *Speech on Slavery.* Delivered at Hamilton City Hall, 7 February, 1851.

Hallam, W. T. *Slave Days in Canada* Toronto: n.p 1919.

Harris, A.M. *A Sketch of the Buxton Mission and Elgin Settlement, Raleigh, Canada West.* Birmingham: J.S. Wilson, 1866.

King William and Robert Burns. *Fugitive Slaves in Canada, Elgin Settlement,* n.p 1860.

Hamilton, James C. *Slavery in Canada* Toronto: n.p, 1890.

Autobiographies and Memoirs

Coffin, Levi. *Reminiscences of Levi Coffin* New York: Arno Press, 1968.

Henson, Josiah. *An Autobiography of the Rev. Josiah Henson From 1789-1876* London: Christian Age Office, 1876.

—. *Father Henson's Story. Story of His Own Life with an Introduction by Mrs H.B Stowe.* Boston: John P. Jewett and Co., 1858.

King, William. *History of the King Family* Delta. Ohio: Atlas Printing Co. 1893.

Loguen, J.W. *The Rev. J.W Loguen, as a Slave and as a Freeman.* Syracuse: J.G.K. Truair and Co., 1859.

Ross, Alexander *Recollections and Experiences of an Abolitionist* Toronto: Roswell and Hutchison, 1876.

Ward, Samuel Ringgold. *Autobiography of a Fugitive Negro.* London: John Snow, 1855.

Warren, Richard. *Narrative of the Life and Sufferings of Rev. Richard Warren (A Fugitive Slave)* Hamilton: Christian Advocate Book and Job Office, 1856.

Unpublished Papers

Green, Adam. "The Future of the Canadian Negro" paper presented at the African Baptist Association, Halifax, Nova Scotia. September 1904.

Roger-Hepburn, Sharon. "The Buxton Settlement: A Community Transformed by the Civil War and Emancipation," paper presented at the Great Lakes History Conference, Michigan, November 2003.

Walker. J. St. G. "On the Other Side of Jordan: The Record of Canada's Black Pioneers 1837-1865," paper presented at the Canadian Historical Association, Annual Meeting, London 1978.

Newspapers and Periodicals

Amherstburg Courier
Amherstburg Echo
Brantford Exposition
Canadian Freeman
Chatham Gleaner
Chatham Journal
Christian Advocate
Christian Freeman
Christian Guardian
Christian Reformer
Citizen
Drayton Advocate
Ecclesiastical and Missionary Record
Evening Times-Globe
Galt Reporter
Globe and Mail
Guelph Mercury
Jamaica Weekly Gleaner
Kent Advertiser
Kitchener-Waterloo Record
Liberator
London Free Press
Missionary Messenger
New York Age
Share
Sun Times
St. Catharines Constitutional
Tri-Weekly Globe

Provincial Freeman
Telegraph-Journal
Voice of the Fugitive
Wellington Advertiser
Windsor Herald

Magazine articles

Blockson, Charles. "Escape from Slavery: The Underground Railroad" *National Geographic* (July 1984): 3-39.

Kelly, Wayne. "Inside Uncle Tom's Cabin" *Heritage Matters* 3. 1 (2005): 2-3.

MacDonald, Cheryl. "Mary Ann Shadd in Canada: Last Stop on the Underground Railroad" *Beaver* (February-March 1990): 32-38.

Teelucksingh, Jerome. "Family History of Early Blacks in Upper Canada" *Families* 38.4 (1999): 233-234.

—. "Coloured Families in Upper Canada 1860-1861" *Families* 41.1 (2002): 33-34.

—. "Upper Canada's Black Presence" *Families* 41.4 (2002): 218-220.

—. "Helpful Theses and Institutions in researching Black Families" *Families* 42. 1 (2003): 43-44.

—. "Secondary Sources to Assist Researchers on Black Families" Families 42.1 (2003): 45-47.

—. "The Bingas: A Coloured Family History" *Families* 42.4 (2003): 237-240

—. "Family Searches in British Methodist Episcopal Church Literature" Families 43.1 (2004): 34.

—. "Family Connections in British Methodist Schools and Churches during 1852" *Families* 43.1 (2004) 35-36.

—. "Family Links with Baptists in the Amherstburg Association during the 1840s" *Families* 43.1 (2004) 37-38.

"The Black Nova Scotian odyssey: a chronology" *Race and Class* 40.1 (1998) 78-91..

Books

Abucar, Mohamed H. *Struggle for Development: The Black Communities of North and East Preston and Cherrybrook, Nova Scotia, 1784-1987.* Dartmouth: Black Cultural Centre for Nova Scotia, 1988.

Akenson, Donald. *The Irish in Ontario- A Study in Rural History.* Montreal: McGill-Queen's University Press, 1984.

Alexander, Ken and Glaze, Avis. *Towards Freedom-The African Canadian Experience.* Toronto: Umbrella Press,1996.

Avery, Donald. *Reluctant Host: Canada's Response to Immigrant Workers 1896-1994.* Toronto: McClelland and Stewart, 1995.

Bartolo, Oswald. *The History of Blacks in Canada: 1608 to Now.* Montreal: National Black Coalition of Canada, 1976.

Bearden, Jim and Linda Jean Butler. *Shadd: The Life and Times of Mary Shadd Cary.* Toronto: N.C. P, 1977.

Bertley, Leo W. *Canada and its People of African Descent.* Pierresfonds, Quebec: Bilongo Publishers, 1970.

Black Cultural Centre of Nova Scotia. *Traditional Lifetime Stories: A Collection of Black Memories.* 2 vols. Dartmouth, Black Cultural Centre for Nova Scotia, 1987 and 1988.

Charles Blockson, *The Underground Railroad: Dramatic Firsthand Accounts of Daring Escapes to Freedom.* New York: Berkley Books, 1994

Blassingame, John. *The Slave Community-Plantation Life in the Antebellum South.* New York: Oxford University Press,1979.

Boyd, Frank Stanley Jr. *A Brief History of the Coloured Baptists of Nova Scotia, 1783-1895.* Halifax: Nova Scotia Department of Education, 1976.

Bramble, Linda *Black Fugitive Slaves in Early Canada.* St. Catharines: Vanwell Publishing, 1988.

Brode, Patrick. *The Odyssey of John Anderson.* Toronto: University of Toronto Press, 1989.

Bruce, David. *And they all sang Hallelujah: Plain-folk camp-meeting religion 1800-1845.* Knoxville, 1974.

Calder, Doris. *All our Born Days: A Lively History of New Brunswick's Kingdom Peninsula.* New Brunswick: Percheron Press, 1984.

Campbell, D. *Banked Fires: The Ethnics of Nova Scotia.* Port Credit, Ontario: Scribbler's P, 1978.

Campbell, Mavis Christine. *The Maroons of Jamaica 1655-1796: A History of Resistance, Collaboration and Betrayal.* Trenton: Africa World Press, 1990.

Carter, Velma. *The Black Canadians: their History and Contributions*. Edmonton: Reidmore, 1989.

Cassidy, Ivan. *Nova Scotia: All About Us*. Scarborough: Nelson Canada, 1983.

Clairmont, Donald H. and Dennis William Magill, *Nova Scotian Blacks: An Historical and Structural Overview*. Halifax: Institute of Public Affairs, Dalhousie University, 1970.

Clayton, Willard Parker. *Whatever Your Will Lord: Emmanuel Baptist Church, Upper Hammonds Plains, Nova Scotia, 1843-1984*. Hansport: Lancelot P, 1984.

Cone, James H. *The Spirituals and the Blues: An interpretation*. New York: Seabury Press, 1972.

Crooks, J.J. *A History of Sierra Leone, Western Africa*. London: n.p., 1903.

Drew, Benjamin. *A North Side View of Slavery. The Refugee: or the Narratives of Fugitive Slaves in Canada*. Boston: John P. Jewett and Co., 1856.

Elgee, William. *The Social Teachings of the Canadian Churches*. Toronto: Ryerson Press, 1964.

Elkins, Stanley. *Slavery - A Problem in American Institutional and Intellectual Life*. Chicago: University of Chicago Press, 1976.

Elgersman, Maureen. *Unyielding Spirits: Black Women and Slavery in Early Canada and Jamaica*. New York: Garland Publishing, 1999.

Everett, Gwen. *John Brown: One man against Slavery*. New York: Rizzoli International Publications, 1993.

Fergusson, C.B. *A Documentary Study of the Establishment of the Negroes in Nova Scotia Between the War of 1812 and the Winning of Responsible Government*. Halifax: Public Archives of Nova Scotia, 1948.

Fergusson, Charles Bruce, ed. *Clarkson's Mission to America, 1791-1792*. Halifax: Public Archives of Nova Scotia, 1971.

French, Gary. *Men of Colour-An Historical Account of the Black Settlement on Wilberforce Street and in Oro Township. Simcoe County, Ontario 1819-1949*. Orilla: Dymet Stubley Printers, 1978.

Fyfe, Christopher. *A History of Sierra Leone*. London: Oxford University, 1962.

—. *Sierra Leone Inheritance*. London: Oxford University, 1964.

Govia, Francine. *Blacks in Canada: in search of the promise*. Edmonton: Harambee Centres, 1988.

Grant, John W. *Profusion of Spires: Religion in Nineteenth Century Ontario*. Toronto: University of Toronto Press, 1988.

Gardiner, James and Roberts, J.D. *Quest for a Black Theology*. Philadelphia: United Church Press, 1971.

Gates Jr. Henry Louis ed. *Spiritual Narratives*. New York: Oxford U Press, 1988.

Gauvreau, Michael. *The Evangelical Century -College and Creed in English Canada from the Great Revival to the Great Depression*. Montreal: McGill-Queen's U Press, 1991.

Goatley, David, E. *Were You There? Godforsakeness in Slave Religion*. New York: Orbis Books, 1996.

Gordon, Grant. *From Slavery to Freedom: The Life of David George, Pioneer Black Baptist Minister*. Hantsport: Lancelot Press, 1992.

Govia, Francine, and Helen Lewis. *Blacks in Canada: A Bibliographical Guide to the History of Blacks in Canada*. Edmonton: Harambee Center, 1988.

Grant, John N. *The Immigration and Settlement of the Black Refugees of the War of 1812 in Nova Scotia and New Brunswick*. Dartmouth: The Black Cultural Centre of Nova Scotia, 1990.

Grant, John. N. *Black Nova Scotians* Halifax: Nova Scotia Museum, 1980.

Greaves, Ida. *The Negro in Canada* Montreal: McGill University Press, 1930.

Harris, A.M. *A Sketch of the Buxton Mission and Elgin Settlement, Raleigh, Canada West*. Alabama, 1866.

Henry, Frances. *Forgotten Canadians: The Blacks of Nova Scotia*. Don Mills, Longmans Canada, 1973.

Hill, Daniel, *The Freedom Seekers: Blacks in Early Canada*. Agincourt: Book Society of Canada, 1981.

Hill, Lawrence. *Trials and Triumph: The Story of African-Canadians*. Toronto: Umbrella Press, 1993.

Hinks, Peter and John McKivigan eds. *Encyclopedia of Antislavery and Abolition* vol. 2 Connecticut: Greenwood Press, 2007.

Hornsby, Jim. *Black Islanders: Prince Edward Island's Historical Black Community*. Charlottetown: Institute of Island Studies, 1991.

Houston, Susan and Prentice, Allison. *Schooling and Scholars in Nineteenth Century Ontario*. Ontario: Historical Board, 1988.

Howe, S.G. *The Refugees from Slavery in Canada West. Report to the Freedmen's Inquiry Commission*. Boston: Wright and Potter, 1864.

Johnson, Alonzo and Jersild, Paul eds. *"Ain't Gonna Lay my 'Ligion Down"-African American Religion in the South*. Columbia, S.C., University of South Carolina Press, 1996.

Charles C. Jones, *The Religious Instruction of the Negroes in the United States*. Savannah, 1842.

Killian, Crawford. *Go Do Some Great Thing: The Black Pioneers of British Columbia*. Vancouver: Douglas & McIntyre, 1978.

Lincoln, Eric. C. *The Black Experience in Religion*. New York: Anchor Press, 1974.

MacKerrow, P.E. *A Brief History of the Coloured Baptists of Nova Scotia, and their First Organisation as Churches, A.D. 1832*. Halifax: Nova Scotia Printing Company, 1895.

Marrant, John. *A Narrative of the Lord's Wonderful Dealings with John Marrant, a Black (Now Going to Preach the Gospel in Nova-Scotia) Born in New-York, in North America*. London: Gilbert & Plummer, 1785.

McDougal, Marion, *Fugitive Slaves (1619-1865)*. New York: Bergman Publishers, 1967.

McIntyre, Paul. *Black Pentecostal Music in Windsor* Ottawa: National Museum of Canada, 1976.

McMullen, Stephanie. *Slavery to Freedom: African Canadians in Grey County*. Owen Sound: Grey County Museum, 2003.

Nova Scotia Human Rights Commission. *Pictorial on Black History in Nova Scotia*. Halifax: International Education Centre, 1974.

Oliver, Pearleen. *An Historic Minority: The Black People of Nova Scotia, 1781-1981*. Dartmouth: Metrographic Printing Services Ltd., 1981.

—. *From Generation to Generation: Bi-Centennial of the Black Church in Nova Scotia, 1785-1985*. Dartmouth: Black Cultural Centre of Nova Scotia, 1986.

—. *A Brief History of the Coloured Baptists of Nova Scotia 1782-1953*. Halifax: African United Baptist Association of Nova Scotia, 1990.

Pachai, Bridglal. *Beneath the Clouds of the Promised Land: The Survival of Nova Scotia's Blacks, 1600-1800*. Halifax: Black Educators Association of Nova Scotia, 1987.

—. *Beneath the Clouds of the Promised Land: The Survival of Nova Scotia Blacks, vol. 2, 1800-1989*. Halifax: Black Educators Association, 1990.

—. *Dr. William Pearley Oliver and the Search for Black Self-Identity in Nova Scotia*. Halifax: International Education Centre, Saint Mary's University, 1979.

Paris, Peter J. *Moral, Political and Religious Significance of the Black Churches in Nova Scotia*. Dartmouth: Black Cultural Centre for Nova Scotia, 1989.

—. *The Moral, Political and Religious Significance of the Black Churches in Nova Scotia* Dartmouth: Black Cultural Centre for Nova Scotia.

Parsons, C G. *Inside View of Slavery: Or a Tour Among the Planters.* Windham: n.p, 1855.

Pease, William and Jane. *Black Utopia.* Madison: State Historical Society of Wisconsin, 1963.

Peterson, John. *Province of Freedom: A Freedom of Sierra Leone, 1787-1870.* London: Faber, 1969.

Petry, Ann Lane. *Harriet Tubman: Conductor on the Underground Railroad.* New York: Harper Trophy, 1996.

Power, Michael and Nancy Butler, *Slavery and Freedom in Niagara.* Niagara-on-the-Lake: Niagara Historical Society, 1993.

Raboteau, Albert J. *Slave Religion -The "Invisible Institution" in the Antebellum South.* New York: Oxford University Press,, 1978.

Rabinowitz, Howard N. *Race Relations in the Urban South 1865-1890.* New York: Oxford University Press, 1978.

Riendeau, Roger E. *An enduring heritage: Black contributions to early Ontario.* Toronto: Dundurn Press, 1984.

Ripley, Peter. *The Black Abolitionist Papers Canada 1830-1865* vol. 2 Chapel Hill: University of North Carolina Press, 1986.

Robertson, J.R. *Landmarks of Toronto: A Collection of Historical Sketches of the Old Town of York From 1792-1837 and of Toronto from 1837-1904* .Toronto: n.p. 1904

Robertson, Marion. *King's Bounty: A History of Early Shelburne.* Halifax: Nova Scotia Museum, 1983.

Robinson, Carey. *The Iron Thorn: The Defeat of the British by the Jamaican Maroons.* Kingston: Kingston Publishers, 1993.

—. *The Fighting Maroons of Jamaica.* Kingston: William Collins & Sangster Ltd., 1969.

Robbins, Arlie. *Legacy to Buxton.* Chatham, Ontario: Ideal Printing, 1983.

Ruck, Calvin. *Canada's Black Battalion, 1916-1920: Canada's Best Kept Military Secret.* Halifax: Nimbus, 1987.

Sadlier, Rosemary. *Harriet Tubman and the Underground Railroad: Her life in the United States and Canada.* Toronto: Umbrella Press,, 1997.

Sanneh, Lamin. *West African Christianity: The Religious Impact.* New York: Orbis, 1983.

Siebert, Wilbur. *The Underground Railroad from Slavery to Freedom.* New York: Russell and Russell, 1899.

Simpson, George Eaton. *Black Religions in the New World* New York: Columbia University Press, 1978.

Arthur L. Smith and Stephen Robbs eds. *The Voice of Black Rhetoric: Selections.* Boston: Allyn and Bacon, 1971.

Smith, Carolyn, et al. *Three Nova Scotia Black Churches: A Collection of Essays*. Dartmouth: Black Cultural Centre of Nova Scotia, 1990.

Smith, T. Watson. "The Slaves of Canada," *Collections of the Nova Scotia Historical Society*, 10 (1899). Reprint. Ottawa: Canadian Institute of Historical Microreproductions, 1985.

Smucker, Barbara. *Underground to Canada*. Toronto: Clarke Irwin, 1977.

Spray, W.A. *The Blacks in New Brunswick*. Fredericton: Brunswick Press, 1972.

Staney, Catherine. *Family Secrets: Crossing the Colour Line*. Toronto: National Heritage Books, 2003.

Steward, Austin. *Twenty-Two Years a Slave and Forty Years a Freeman*. New York: William Alling, 1857.

Still, William. *The Underground Railroad*. Philadelphia: Porter and Coates, 1872.

Talbot, Carol. *Growing Up Black in Canada*. Toronto: Williams-Wallace Productions, 1984.

Thomas, Owen. *Niagara's Freedom Trail: Guide to African-Canadian History on the Niagara Peninsula*. Niagara: Niagara Tourist Council, 1995.

Thompson, Alvin. *Flight to Freedom: African Runaways and Maroons in the Americas*, Jamaica: University of the West Indies Press, 2006.

Thomson, Colin A. *Blacks in Deep Snow -Black Pioneers in Canada*. Don Mills: J.M Dent and Sons, 1979.

Tower, Philo. *Slavery Unmasked : being a truthful narrative of a three years' residence and journeying in eleven Southern States: to which is added the invasion of Kansas, including the last chapter of her wrongs*. New York: E. Darrow and Brother, 1856.

Troy, William. *Hair-Breath Escapes for Slavery to Freedom*. Manchester: n.p, 1861.

Tulloch, Headley. *Black Canadians*. Toronto: N.C. P, 1975.

Ullman, Victor. *Look to the North Star: A Life of William King*. Boston: Beacon Press, 1969.

Voegeli, Jacque. *Free But Not Equal*. Chicago: University of Chicago Press, 1967.

Walker, James W. St. G. *The Black Loyalists: The Search for a Promised Land in Nova Scotia and Sierra Leone, 1783-1870*. Halifax: Dalhousie University Press, 1976.

—. *A History of Blacks in Canada: A Study Guide for Teachers and Students*. Hull, Quebec: Minister of State for Multiculturalism, 1980.

—. *Racial Discrimination in Canada: The Black Experience*. Ottawa: Canadian Historical Association Booklet, 1985.

—. *Black Identity in Nova Scotia: Community and Institutions in Historical Perspectives.* Dartmouth: Black Cultural Centre of Nova Scotia, 1985.

Walls, William. *The African Methodist Episcopal Zion Church-Reality of the Black Church.* North Carolina: A.M.E.Z Publishing House, 1974.

Westfall, William. *Two Worlds- The Protestant Culture of Nineteenth - Century Ontario.* Montreal: McGill-Queen's University Press, 1989.

Winks, Robin. *The Blacks in Canada- A History.* Montreal: McGill-Queen's University Press, 1977.

Zucchi, John *Italians in Toronto-Development of a National Identity 1875-1895.* Montreal: McGill-Queen's University Press, 1988.

Journals

Beaton, Elizabeth. "The African-American Community in Cape Breton, 1901-1904," *Acadiensis* 2 (Spring 1995): 65-97.

Barry Cahill, "Stephen Blucke: The Perils of Being a "White Negro" in Loyalist Nova Scotia," *Nova Scotia Historical Review* 11 (1991): 129-134.

Caven, William, "The Rev. Michael Willis," *Knox College Monthly* 11 (January 1886): 97-101.

Epps, Archie, C. "The Christian doctrine of Slavery: A Theological Analysis," *Journal of Negro History* 46 (October 1961): 243-249.

Farrell, John. "Schemes for the Transplanting of Refugee American Negroes from Upper Canada in the 1840s," *Ontario History* 52 (December 1960): 245-250.

Fingard, Judith. "From Sea to Rail: Black Transportation Workers and Their Families in Halifax, c. 1870-1916," *Acadiensis* 2 (Spring 1995): 49-64.

Grant, John N. "Black Immigrants into Nova Scotia, 1776-1815," *Journal of Negro History* 3 (July 1973): 253-270.

Green, Ernest. "Upper Canada's Black Defenders," *Ontario Historical Society Papers and Records* 25 (1931): 365-391.

Hamilton, J.C. "The African in Canada," *Knox College Monthly* 11 (November 1889): 30-33.

Hill, Daniel. "Negroes in Toronto 1793-1865," *Ontario History* 55 (June 1963): 73-92.

Hite, Roger W. "Voice of a Fugitive: Henry Bibb and Ante-bellum Black Separatism," *Journal of Black Studies* 4 (March 1974): 269-284.

Landon, Fred. "The History of the Wilberforce Refugee Colony in Middlesex County," *Transactions of the London and Middlesex Society* Part 9 (1918): 30-44.

—. "Canada's Part in Freeing the Slave," *Ontario Historical Society Papers and Records* 17 (1919): 74-83.

—. "Henry Bibb, a Colonizer," *Journal of Negro History* 5 (October 1920): 437-447.

—. "The Negro Migration to Canada After the Passing of the Fugitive Slave Act," *Journal of Negro History* 5 (January 1920): 22-36.

—. "Social Conditions among the Negroes in Upper Canada Before 1865," *Ontario Historical Society Papers and Records* 12 (1925): 144-161.

—. "The Anti-Slavery Society of Canada," *Journal of Negro History* 4 (January 1919): 33-40.

Law, Howard. "Self-Reliance is the True Road to Independence: Ideology and the Ex-Slaves in Buxton and Chatham," *Ontario History* 77 (June 1985): 107-121.

Lockett, James. "The Deportation of the Maroons of Trelawny Town to Nova Scotia, Then Back to Africa," *Journal of Black Studies* 30 (September 1999): 5-14.

Lubka, Nancy. "Ferment in Nova Scotia," *Queen's Quarterly* 2 (1969): 213-228.

Martin, Ged. "British Officials and their Attitudes to the Negro Community in Canada 1833-1861," *Ontario History* 66 (June 1974): 79-88.

Moreau, Bernice. "Black Nova Scotian Women's Experience of Educational Violence in the early 1900s: A Case of Colour Contusion," *Dalhousie Review* (Summer 1997): 179-206.

Paris, Peter J. "The Spirituality of African Peoples," *Dalhousie Review* 73 (Fall 1973): 294-307.

Pease, William H. and Jane Pease. "Opposition to the Founding of the Elgin Settlement," *Canadian Historical Review* 38 (1957): 202-218.

Posey, Walter. B. "The Baptists and Slavery in the Lower Mississippi Valley," *Journal of Negro History* 43 (July, 1957): 201-213.

Rawlyk, G.A. "The Guysborough Negroes: A Study in Isolation," *Dalhousie Review* 48 (Spring 1968): 24-36.

Raymond, Charles. "The Religious Life of the Negro Slave," *Harper's Magazine* 28 (September 1863): 479-485.

Riddell, William Renwick. "Notes on Slavery in Canada," *Journal of Negro History* 4 (October 1919): 396-411.

—. "Slavery in Canada," *Journal of Negro History* 5 (July 1920): 261-377.

—. "Some References to Negroes in Upper Canada," *Ontario History* (1925): 144-145.

—. "Notes on the Slave in Nouvelle-France," *Journal of Negro History* (July 1923): 316-330.

Shanks, Caroline L. "The Biblical Anti-Slavery Argument of the Decade 1830-1840," *Journal of Negro History* 16 (April 1931): 132-157.

Silverman, Jason and Gillie, Donna. "The Pursuit of Knowledge Under Difficulties": Education and the Fugitive Slave in Canada," *Ontario History* 74 (June 1982): 95-112

Stouffer, Allen P. "'A Restless Child of Change and Accident': The Black Image in Nineteenth Century Ontario," *Ontario History* 76 (June 1984): 128-150.

Walker, James St. G. "Allegories and Orientations in African-Canadian Historiography: The Spirit of Africville," *Dalhousie Review* (Summer 1997): 155-178.

Winks, Robin. "Negro School Segregation in Ontario and Nova Scotia," *Canadian Historical Review* 50 (1969):164-191.

—. "Negroes in the Maritimes: An Introductory Survey," *Dalhousie Review* 48 (Winter 1968-69): 453-476.

INDEX